The Plagiarism Handbook

Strategies for Preventing, Detecting, and Dealing with Plagiarism

Robert A. Harris

Vanguard University of Southern California

Cartoons by Vic Lockman
based on ideas by the author.

 Pyrczak Publishing

P.O. Box 39731 • Los Angeles, CA 90039

Visit us at www.AntiPlagiarism.com

Although the author and publisher have made every effort to ensure the accuracy and completeness of information contained in this book, we assume no responsibility for errors, inaccuracies, omissions, or any inconsistency herein. Any slights of people, places, or organizations are unintentional. No information or opinions in this book should be construed as legal advice.

Editorial assistance provided by Brenda Koplin, Elaine Parks, Sharon Young, Cheryl Alcorn, Monica Lopez, and Randall R. Bruce.

Cover design by Robert Kibler and Larry Nichols.

Printed in the United States of America.

ISBN 1-884585-35-3

Contents

Notes:

Introduction

> There are free databases of papers just waiting for you to download. You can use someone's paper from across the country and not have to worry about the teacher recognizing the piece of writing. If you want to compose your own paper, the Internet also makes it easier to cut and paste information; you do not even have to retype the text. The joy of the Internet is that your spliced paper can come from all over the world and be virtually untraceable.
>
> – Maria Stroffolino
> "How to Plagiarize Papers
> Off the Internet"

This book is for everyone who is disturbed by the above quotation, which appeared in a university student newspaper. More specifically, this book is for everyone who assigns, helps students with, or grades research papers, and who is looking for practical tools and ideas to combat plagiarism. Graduate student teaching assistants facing their first class, new professors designing writing requirements, and even veteran professors looking for another idea or two should all benefit from this book. Those who assist classroom professors, such as reference librarians and support staff, will also find the book useful. While the book's primary focus is at the undergraduate college level, it should be helpful as well to high school teachers and concerned parents who help their children with their homework. Plagiarism has become easier because of the advent of electronic databases and the Internet, and more common, not just because of a rise in intentional cheating but also because of a growing lack of awareness of the proper use of research sources. To fight these trends, new approaches for prevention and detection must be added to the traditional ones; and the earlier such preventive knowledge, tools, and education can be obtained, the more likely the problem can be controlled.

Do you need this book?

How much of a problem is plagiarism? Some of the findings are informative:

- One free-term-paper site, run by a 16-year-old, receives 13,000 hits a day (Clayton, 1997).

- A librarian who went undercover to investigate plagiarism ordered a paper from a term paper mill. The paper could not be delivered on time because the site was being flooded with 800 orders a day (Bushweller, 1999).
- A study of several hundred undergraduates revealed that their ignorance about the rules for quoting and citing indicates that "the majority of students probably engage in inadvertent plagiarism" by the way they handle borrowed material (Roig, 1997).
- Despite warning his class in advance that he would be checking their papers for signs of plagiarism, Berkeley professor David Presti found that 45 out of 300 papers submitted had at least some sections copied from other sources (Kelly, 2000).
- John Barrie, one of the founders of Plagiarism.org, says the company's detection service is experiencing a 10 to 15 percent plagiarism rate on papers it checks (Mayfield, 1999).
- In a class on information security at George Washington University during fall 1997, graduate teaching assistant Julie J.C.H. Ryan discovered that seven of her 42 students plagiarized "most or all" of their papers (Ryan, 1998).
- A former tutor at the University of Minnesota admitted to having written "400 academic papers for members of the men's basketball team" (Reed, 1999).

How will this book help?

Plagiarism is a complex issue that arises from several factors including ignorance, opportunity, technology, changes in ethical values, competitive pressures, perceived lack of consequences, and even poorly designed assignments. To reduce plagiarism, then, a multifaceted approach is needed. This book provides ways to reduce plagiarism from several angles.

- Chapter 1 covers the causes of plagiarism and cheating, and provides practical suggestions for attacking these causes. It also describes many of the types of plagiarism and concludes by asking you to think about plagiarism in the context of personal and institutional values and practices.
- Chapter 2 offers material to help educate students about plagiarism so that the amount of unintentional plagiarism can be greatly reduced. The chapter also provides some philosophical and ethical content for discussing with students why plagiarism is wrong and why citing sources actually strengthens their writing.

- Chapter 3 presents many suggestions for constructing research paper assignments that will produce papers highly resistant to plagiarizing. Adopting some of the ideas in this chapter should greatly reduce the amount of intentional plagiarism in the papers turned in to you.
- Chapter 4 covers strategies for detecting plagiarism. The standard clues are covered for the benefit of new paper graders, and some more subtle ones are also included for the practiced eye. Information on term paper mills and on searching electronic databases and the Internet is included, together with a list and discussion of commercial detection software and services.
- Chapter 5 discusses the various means of handling a case of plagiarism once it has been identified. Strategies are presented to help you obtain a confession when your evidence is too circumstantial for conviction. Some recommendations are also given for institutional policy and practice.
- Chapter 6 covers policy issues that should be discussed and decided at the institutional and administrative level. It is crucial that processes surrounding the punishment of plagiarism be just, fair, and equitable. Students' rights and due process must be respected, the administration needs to support faculty efforts to combat the problem, and the faculty should operate within administrative policy. These goals can be accomplished only if everyone has a hand in establishing clear and workable systems.
- The Appendices provide lists and discussions of tools and examples to support your antiplagiarism work. Included are sample definitions and policies, quizzes and activities, reproducible handouts with examples of acceptable and unacceptable use of sources, lists of search tools for locating suspect texts on-line, and lists of term paper mills.
- Twenty-four reproducible cartoons presenting various issues surrounding plagiarism are included in the book. These cartoons are supported by ideas for using them in teaching and discussion about the subject. (See Appendix G.)

In a word, then, the goal of the book is to provide you with a tool kit of resources for fighting this unfortunate cancer in the body of academe.

Permission to reproduce.

Individual instructors who own a copy of this book are granted permission to use the cartoons in the book and the instructional materials in Appendices B and C in their classroom instruction with their students. Permissible uses are making overhead transparencies or photocopies (up to one per student enrolled in the instructor's course) or projecting the materials onscreen in class. All reproduced materials should bear the notice "Copyright 2001 by Pyrczak Publishing. All rights reserved. Reproduced with permission." Please see the copyright notice on page *ii* for further details.

Ideas and anecdotes are welcome.

The author welcomes all ideas you may have, together with anecdotes related to assignments, detecting, or dealing with cases of plagiarism. Please write to the author in care of the publisher.

Disclaimer.

The author and publisher believe that this book provides useful and effective advice. However, since the specific application of any ideas here is beyond our control, you must use your own discretion in what you do and take responsibility for the outcome. The publisher and author do not warrant the efficacy of the tools and strategies discussed in this book. Mention of specific software or services is for reference only and does not necessarily constitute a recommendation or guarantee of performance. Nothing said here should be understood as a substitute for competent legal counsel or as a recommendation to circumvent established policies or processes at your institution. No fees or other considerations were received in exchange for mention of any sites, software, or services in this book.

Acknowledgments.

Thanks to Fred Pyrczak, acquisition editor, publisher, supplier of many ideas, and supporter throughout the project.

Thanks to Susan Nylander for her research assistance.

Thanks to Shirley Albertson Owens, Murray Dempster, Rob Nelson, Linda Edlund, Paula Miller, Kristina Petrosino, Amanda Speelman, Zachary Stred, Desiree Turnbow, Andrew Yeager, Julia Johansen, Karla Yatckoske, and Charity Cedarholm for their contributions of anecdotes.

Robert A. Harris

Chapter 1

Educating Yourself About Plagiarism

Every generation has the privilege of standing on the shoulders of the generation that went before; but it has no right to pick the pockets of the first-comer.

– Brander Matthews
Recreations of an Anthologist

The proverb tells us that "forewarned is forearmed." A first step toward combating the rise in plagiarism is to understand what causes students to submit to the temptation. This chapter explains the many and varied reasons behind this cheating, together with suggested remedies or preventions for each of the causes. "Prevention is the best cure," another proverb tells us, and it is the goal of this chapter, and a principal thrust of the entire book, to help remedy the plagiarism scourge by applying preventive measures wherever possible. The second section of the chapter discusses the varieties of plagiarism, from downloading an entire paper to the fabrication of sources. This section also includes brief comments about how to detect each kind of theft. The final section of the chapter asks you to engage in a little introspection to determine your own thoughts and philosophy about plagiarism and how committed you are to fighting it.

✓ 1.1 UNDERSTAND WHY STUDENTS CHEAT.

Students plagiarize for a wide variety of reasons. By understanding some of the reasons, and applying appropriate preventatives, you can take steps to prevent cheating by attacking the causes. Some of the major reasons include the following.

1.1.1 Ignorance.

A recent study among several hundred undergraduates revealed widespread uncertainty about what exactly constitutes plagiarism. Perhaps the most dramatic finding was that "as long as the original author is acknowledged, many students seem to believe that it is proper to take portions of text, with little or no modification, and to appropriate such text as their own writing" (Roig, 1997). In one part of the study, 65 percent of the students judged a particular passage (which had been copied with very few changes) not to have been plagiarized simply because the author had been referred to, even absent a citation. Such lack of understanding about what actually constitutes plagiarism indicates that "the majority of students probably engage in inadvertent plagiarism." Many professors have had students submit papers with a long paragraph or series of related paragraphs that contain a citation either at the very end, in Modern Language Association (MLA) style, or at the very beginning, in American Psychological Association (APA) style, but with no indication about what portion of the paragraph the citation is intended to cover. This may be indicative of ignorance about the rules of citation.

The best way to overcome confusion and uncertainty is to supply students with a variety of examples, including appropriate and inappropriate uses. See Chapter 2 for further discussion and Appendix C for examples of proper and improper use of sources.

1.1.2 Careless note taking.

Students often work in haste, and when they do, they sometimes do not clearly distinguish between a quotation, a paraphrase, or their own commentary. Such confusion can obviously lead to accidental plagiarism. Just as obviously, such a reason can be a facile excuse for the student who has been caught stealing words. The way out of this difficulty is to teach careful note taking. See Chapter 2, Section 2.2.2, for further information.

"Must be working on her research paper.
I keep hearing her mumbling, 'Edit, copy, edit,
paste!'"

Notice: Please see the copyright notice on page *ii* for limited permission to reprint the cartoons. See Appendix G for teaching suggestions.

1.1.3 Stress and competition.

Some students are tempted to take shortcuts because of the pressures of workloads, course difficulty, competition to get into graduate school, and even shortness of time now that so many students work part-time to help get themselves through school. There is no easy solution to this problem other than to be as supportive as possible. You might invite students to come to your office if they have particular pressure problems, be a little flexible as appropriate with deadlines, and avoid making any one assignment more than, say, 20 percent of the entire course grade. Students facing a "make or break" research paper that counts as half the course grade may buckle under the pressure.

1.1.4 Lack of buy-in to the educational enterprise.

Many students are simply not convinced that the hard work required for a real education is worth it. The reasons may be manifold. Some students believe that the diploma will be a magic ticket to a high-paying job regardless of what they learn, so that all the shortcuts they can find are appropriate. Some students go to college just to find a mate. Some students are attending college somewhat unwillingly, sent there at the insistence of their parents. Some go to college to be with their friends. And so on. The result is something like the college population of the late sixties and early seventies, where many students attended just to get a military draft deferment: Some students simply do not like academic work. An inkling of these feelings can be discerned in the names of some of the paper mill sites: Schoolsucks.com, Screwschool.com, Schoolbytes.com, and so on, a few even worse.

Students with antieducation attitudes can sometimes be brought around by discussions of the purpose of education, by creating assignments they find interesting, and by developing a working relationship with them (invite them to your office to explore their interests and perhaps find a topic as a result). As Anecdote

1.1.4.1 below shows, students who feel unjustly restricted or bullied are more likely to be tempted to plagiarize just to get the assignment—which they now dislike—completed.

Anecdote 1.1.4.1

One time I was tempted to plagiarize a paper in my Critical Thinking English class. We had an assignment to watch a movie called *The People vs. Larry Flynt*. I told the professor that I wouldn't watch it due to the sexually explicit content in it and asked for an alternative. She got very frustrated with me and wouldn't look at it from my point of view and proceeded to assign me a 10-page research paper on the 13th Amendment which was due in three days. Due to the fact that I was balancing a workload of 18 units at that time, there was no way I could have gotten that done. I was very tempted to plagiarize a paper to get by in that class. Instead, I decided to drop the class because my teacher was unfairly discriminating against me.

– Amanda Speelman, university junior

1.1.5 Tutoring out of control.

Even before computers, some paper typists offered quite a bit of help to students, fixing punctuation and spelling errors. Word processors now often take care of many of the spelling issues, but tutors are sometimes even more helpful than the typists used to be by fixing grammar, sentence structure, and in some cases, virtually writing assignments for the student.

Weak students need help, but they need help in learning to perform by themselves. Having their work done for them is actually a disservice. Tutoring centers and tutors need to be brought into the equation by administrators and faculty and educated about their roles. Perhaps clearly written institutional policy needs to be developed as part of the entire academic dishonesty policy set.

As an immediate approach, you might discuss with students, either in class or on an individual basis, what kind of help they are and are not permitted to receive from tutors, the writing center, or other support areas. Remember that weaker students need encouragement, and it is human nature for many of us to want to sit back and watch a superior performer work on a task that we were fumbling.

> Give a man a fish, and he will have food for a day; teach
> him how to fish, and he will have food for many days.
>
> – Proverb

1.1.6 Cheating in self-defense.

In a study of six thousand students in United States colleges and universities, researchers discovered that "the perception of peers' behavior was the most influential contextual variable" in the rate of cheating (McCabe and Trevino, 1993, p. 533). The researchers concluded that not only does the behavior of one's fellow students create "a kind of normative support for cheating" but "the fact that others are cheating may also suggest that . . . the non-cheater feels left at a disadvantage" (p. 533). Cheating in self-defense may appear rational in a highly competitive atmosphere, especially where students believe there are few operative punishments.

1.1.7 Perceived cheating by authority figures.

Logical fallacies are still taught because many people still fall for them. The fallacy of *tu quoque* ("you're doing it so I can, too") is sometimes used by students as an excuse to cheat. They see those in role model positions—from parents to politicians, from businessmen to bureaucrats—lying, cheating, covering up, and even plagiarizing (recent cases involving novelists, scholars, even academic deans have come to light). In a society that appears to be morally adrift even at the upper levels, where absolutes are dismissed as arbitrary constructions, some students think that honesty is for suckers.

Responding to this attitude can be a challenge. If you teach at a religiously affiliated school, you can make an appeal to shared or timeless values and to the standards included in the faith commitment. In a public university, you can declare your own ethical standards and expectations and work with students to develop their own internalized ethical codes. See Chapter 2 for further information and advice on raising ethical questions to help students with being honest.

1.1.8 Lack of perceived punishment.

You may be familiar with Lawrence Kohlberg's theory of moral development and the stages he says people pass through on their way to moral maturity. Judging by the increasing number of people who run red lights or try to swindle e-commerce sites, a significant portion of society is regressing to Kohlberg's "preconventional" stage, where the behavioral determiner is "punishment is bad." This determiner appears to supply the operational principle for those students who cheat because they do not believe they will be caught. Some students have the attitude that "no one cares," so they feel justified. Others believe that "everyone else is cheating and no one is doing anything about it," so they, too, must cheat simply to keep up with the competition. According to a report from the U. S. Department of Education, some studies show that students are less likely to cheat when professors make clear that detection and punishment are operational (Maramark & Maline, 1993).

1.1.9 Students are natural economizers.

Many students are interested in the shortest route possible through a course. That's why they ask questions such as, "Will this be on the test?" Copying a paper sometimes looks like a shortcut through an assignment, especially when students feel overloaded with work already. To combat this cause, assign your paper to be due well before the end-of-term pressures. Remind students that the purpose of the course is to learn and to develop skills and not just to "get through." The more they learn and develop their skills, the more effective they will be in their future lives.

1.1.10 Students are faced with too many choices, so they put off low priorities.

With so many things to do (both of academic and recreational nature), many students put off assignments that do not interest them. A remedy is to allow each student to select a topic of personal interest from the subject area the instructor wants covered or to offer topics with high intrinsic interest to the student. Topics connected to students' lives beyond the classroom can also provide effective ways to garner and maintain interest.

1.1.11 Many students have poor time management and planning skills.

Some students are just procrastinators, while others underestimate the hours required to develop a good research paper, so they run out of time as the due date looms. Thus, they are most tempted to copy a paper when time is short and they have not yet started the assignment. If you structure your research assignment so that intermediate parts of it (for example, topic, early research, prospectus, outline, draft, bibliography, final draft) are due at regular intervals, students will be less likely to get into a time-pressure panic and look for an expedient shortcut.

1.1.12 Some students fear that their writing ability is inadequate.

Fear of a bad grade and inability to perform cause some students to look for a superior product. Ironically, these students are among those least able to judge a good paper and are often likely to turn in a very poor copied one. Some help for these students may come from demonstrating how poor many of the papers available on the Internet are and by emphasizing the value of the learning process (more on this below). Reassuring students of the help available to them (your personal attention, a writing center, teaching assistants, on-line writing lab sites, etc.) may give them the courage to persevere.

1.1.13 Some students do not believe professors actually read research papers.

Too many research papers are turned back without a mark on them other than the grade—no questions or comments in the margins, no marked misspellings, not even an occasional notation of "good point" in the margin, and no evaluative comments at the end. To the student, these facts are evidence that the paper has not been read. If the professor is not going to read the paper, why put in an honest effort? (This self-defeating student logic is not healthy, of course, but that is how many students think.)

The fact is, a paper simply due at the end of the term and returned without comments will not only provide a temptation to plagiarism but will also produce a poor learning experience because of a lack of feedback. Grant Wiggins (1993), writing about feedback in educational systems, notes that no one gets good at anything without feedback. We have to adjust our performance based on intermediate outcomes, which in writing, means feedback on ideas, outlines, and especially, drafts. As Wiggins notes, it is the student's attempt to do something and get feedback on the degree of success that results in learning (Chapter 6).

"Oh, bad luck! Missed an 'A' by a quarter of an ounce!"

How some students think instructors grade papers.

Anecdote 1.1.13.1

As an eighth grade teacher, I am savvy enough to assign papers and projects that require thinking and varied responses, not just a standard report. One of the saddest remarks was made in my science class last year when a student plagiarized his paper for the science fair. After I gave him a zero and talked with him about what he'd done (and yes, I'd addressed the issue many times), he said to me that no other teacher had said anything to him about this. (This was not his first time.) My comment? I said with great sorrow that maybe it was because no teacher had ever really read what he had written. Unfortunately, many teachers assign papers and never really read them.

– Linda Edlund, eighth grade English teacher

1.1.14 A few students like the thrill of rule breaking.

The more angrily you condemn plagiarism, the more some students can hardly wait to engage in it. An approach that may have some effect is to present the assignment and the proper citation of sources in a positive light (more below).

1.1.15 Cryptomnesia.

Cryptomnesia or unconscious plagiarism has been shown to occur when thinkers forget to monitor their sources closely. Ideas they have read or heard become assimilated into their pool of thought and later emerge under the guise of original ideas. Instances of cryptomnesia are most likely to be seen as the copying of apt phrases or ideas.

Cryptomnesia is probably more common now than before and will likely increase for three reasons. First, there are more people working with information than ever before. Our information economy depends on millions of knowledge workers. Second, the quantity of information each person must process each day or year seems to be increasing almost geometrically. Many people complain about the growth of their e-mail volume, the number of journal articles they should be reading, and how far behind they feel. Richard Saul Wurman (1989) has written about the "information anxiety" that some people experience when faced with the quantity of information they feel obligated to consume and process. Third, information comes to us from more sources than ever, further complicating the sourcing issue through an increasing attribution ambiguity. Not only are there more books and journals, but more Web sites, news groups, listserves, e-mails, and so on. It is no wonder that we seem to say more often, "I think I read somewhere that. . . ."

The implications of this for students is that if they engage in heavy research (as, say, graduate students do), they may be setting themselves up for cryptomnesic plagiarism unless they very carefully record and track every source. Similarly, foreign students from cultures that emphasize memorization as the principal learning method may be more likely to commit this accidental plagiarism as they are, in effect, copying from memory without recalling the source ("Foreign Students," 1998).

1.1.16 Previous education at odds with university standards.

Both foreign and American students occasionally reveal that the way they have been taught to use sources conflicts dramatically with the standards for use and citation at the university. Whether it is a foreign student who has been taught that copying the source verbatim "honors the writer," or the local student who was taught in high school to present only the ideas of sources because the student's ideas "did not matter," you may discover that some re-education is in order. A profitable watchword may be, "Do not presume ignorance; presume miseducation."

Anecdote 1.1.16.1

While I was in high school my teachers asked me to put cites after every paragraph that we used outside information from, regardless of how much of it was our own or not.

– Paula Miller, university freshman

✓ 1.2 UNDERSTAND THE VARIETIES OF PLAGIARISM.

Plagiarism on research papers takes many forms. Some students plagiarize from ignorance or confusion, while others know exactly what they are doing. Some of the most common types of plagiarism include the following.

1.2.1 Downloading a free research paper.

Perhaps the most glaring and abhorrent form of plagiarism involves downloading an entire paper from one of the sites offering free papers. There are scores of these sites (see Appendix E) with a combined collection of tens of thousands of papers. Many of these papers have been written and shared by other students responding to various research assignments, so many of the papers include citations and a bibliography. However, because paper swappers are often not among the best students, and because some of them are high school students, the free papers are often of poor quality, in both mechanics and content. Some of the papers are surprisingly old (with citations being no more recent than the seventies). See Chapter 2, Section 2.3, for some ideas on helping students understand why this kind of cheating is so offensive.

1.2.2 Buying a paper from a commercial paper mill.

If you are incensed by students who care so little about your assignment or their education that they hand in some old paper they could get free from a mill site, what do you think of the student who substitutes cash for learning and buys a paper from a commercial mill site? These papers can be good—and sometimes they are too good. One advantage of giving an occasional in-class writing assignment is that if you encounter a paper that is suspiciously well written, you can compare it with the in-class essay and be quite enlightened. Moreover, mills often sell both custom and stock papers, with custom papers becoming stock papers very quickly. If you visit some of the mill sites, you might find the same paper already offered for sale even if the student had it written as a custom product.

Visiting some of the sites that give away or sell research papers can be an informative experience. If you have Web projection capability, you might visit selected sites in class and show the students (1) that you know about these sites and (2) that the papers are often well below your expectations for quality, research, and timeliness. If you do not have projection capability, you might make an overhead transparency of a paper or two to use in discussing the kinds of papers available. There is a list of many paper mill sites in Appendix E, with notations about which ones have free papers.

1.2.3 Copying an article from the Web or an on-line or electronic database.

Another form of computer-aided information theft is the copying of an on-line article and submitting it as the student's own. Only some of these articles will have the quantity and type of citations that academic research papers are expected to have. If you receive a well-written, highly informed essay without a single citation (or with just a few), it may have been copied wholesale from an electronic source. On the other hand, you may receive a sophisticated, well-footnoted article that reminds you of a scholarly journal article. Because there are many on-line journals and many commercial databases with electronic versions of print journals, the highly sophisticated paper may indeed be a journal article. A third form of plagiarized work involves adding a list of faked citations to a copied article that lacked citations or a bibliography. See Section 1.2.11 for more information.

1.2.4 Translating a foreign Web article into English.

A particularly sneaky technique is for a student to find an article on the Web in a foreign language, such as French, German, or Italian, and then use one of the on-line translators, such as AltaVista's Babelfish (http://babelfish.altavista.com), to translate it into English (Stebelman, 1998). The student will then need to do some substantial touching up of the language and syntax, but the result will be difficult to trace. For some time now, language students have been using translation software to do their homework, so this development should not be surprising. The most profitable detection method for a translation case is to look at the citations. Even if their titles have been translated to English, the journal names may still be foreign, or the English translation of the journal names may be journals that do not exist. Checking a citation or two might be highly informative.

1.2.5 Copying a paper from a local source.

Papers may be copied from students who have taken your course previously, from fraternity files, or from other paper-sharing sources near campus. If you keep copies of papers previously turned in to you, they can be a source of detection of this particular practice. It is common for students to lend their computer disks or to e-mail a copy of a paper to a friend to "look at" what was written for the same or a similar course. The lender may feel honest because he or she is just showing the paper as an example. The borrower, under whatever pressure or temptation, then often copies whole paragraphs or even the entire paper. A good way to eliminate the "he said, she said" complications of this kind of copying is to prohibit explicitly both the lending and the borrowing of disks or papers.

Remember, too, that the old-fashioned method of copying a paper out of a printed source has gone high-tech with the common availability of scanners and optical character recognition (OCR) software. Do not ignore printed books and journals as possible sources of text.

1.2.6 Cutting and pasting to create a paper from several sources.

Some students create a paper by taking a paragraph here and a paragraph there and pasting them all together into an essay. These "assembly-kit" papers are often betrayed by wide variations in tone, diction, and citation style. The introduction and conclusion are often student-written and therefore noticeably different from and weaker than the often-glowing middle. Through the years, many students who have not understood the research paper process have written papers consisting of little more than block quotations, connected by a few sparse comments. In such papers, the only original thinking has often been, "Jones says," "On the other hand, Smith asserts," and "Of course, this is complicated by Brown, who notes," and so on. The fully plagiarized version of these papers simply presents the texts without introductions or quotation marks. Students who do not realize that their own thinking is the goal of the research paper may be more likely to fall into this kind of plagiarism. If they are told that the quotations, paraphrases, and summaries should support *their* arguments and the points *they* are developing, then they may begin to see that merely presenting research material is not the goal.

1.2.7 Quoting less than all the words copied.

This practice includes premature end quotation marks or missing quotation marks. A common type of plagiarism occurs when a student quotes a sentence or two, places the end quotation mark and the citation, and then continues copying from the source. Or the student may copy from the source verbatim without any quotation marks at all, but add a citation, implying that the information is the student's summary of the source. In the most insidious form, the student may introduce a quotation and include the opening quotation mark, but omit the closing mark. The actual quotation (or copying) may continue for several sentences or even for the rest of the paragraph. This tactic allows an entire paragraph to be plagiarized, and if caught, the student can claim simply to have accidentally left off the closing quotation mark. Checking the citation will expose all three forms of this practice of premature end or missing quotation marks. As mentioned earlier, education is the best prevention for this practice, since it is often committed out of ignorance.

1.2.8 Changing some words but copying whole phrases.

Some students will change a few words here and there, either better to match their own vocabulary or to disguise the fact that they are copying from a source. Or perhaps they believe that by making a few alterations they are changing the text into their own words, thereby making it their own. As mentioned above, many of these examples will include the citation with them. This category of plagiarism is the most likely to be inadvertent or performed with good intentions, and is best addressed by educating the students about appropriate and inappropriate paraphrasing. See Appendices B and C for helpful quizzes and teaching resources that will provide guidance to students in this area.

1.2.9 Paraphrasing without attribution.

Paraphrasing is the conversion of some amount of text (usually a sentence or paragraph) into different words without shortening the text. In other words, a paraphrase simply turns a statement into different words. As with the practice of changing only some words (mentioned above), paraphrasing without including a citation is either an attempt to make the thought content appear to be the student's own, or is done with the mistaken belief that the idea is now lawfully the student's.

1.2.10 Summarizing without attribution.

A summary is the conversion of text into fewer words than are present in the original, thus condensing it. What some students do not understand is that the idea itself, expressed however briefly, is in need of citation, so that a summary does not preclude the necessity of citing the source of the idea.

1.2.11 Faking a citation.

In lieu of real research, some students will make up quotations, evidence, or data and supply fake citations. You can discover this practice by randomly checking citations. If you require several Web or other electronic sources for the paper, these can be checked quickly. Many journal citations can be checked through your library's subscription to on-line databases. Cited books can sometimes be checked by reading the reviews and commentary about the books in order to determine whether a particular book does indeed cover the subject claimed by the citation (Ryan, 1998). On-line bookstores such as Amazon.com have reviews, summaries, and sometimes sample chapters. *The New York Times* has more than 50,000 book reviews on-line. See Appendix D, Section D.5, for a list of other sources and Web addresses (URLs).

"All right, Sir. With your coupon for buy two, get one free, that's three causes of the Russian Revolution for $54 ²⁵! If you need a somewhat longer paper, you might be interested in our special promotional offer of two additional causes for only $19 ²⁵ more!"

✓ 1.3 UNDERSTAND THE PERSONAL AND POLITICAL REALITIES OF THE BATTLE.

An important part of your own education about plagiarism comes from examining yourself and your own feelings about your commitment to teaching the research process, keeping an eye out

19

for possible cheating, and following through when you find evidence of plagiarism. From a pragmatic standpoint, you should learn where your department and administration stand on the issue, both in theory and in practice.

1.3.1 How interested are you in teaching the research paper process?

Teaching students how to research a topic, work with sources, analyze issues, and present a coherent argument is a crucial part of education and training in thinking. However, the process is labor intensive for the professor, especially if multiple steps and drafts are required. On top of that, the library or research paper is the most prone to plagiarism and hence the most likely to produce the psychic trauma involved with detecting and punishing it. You should therefore think about these issues, and if you are assigning a research paper simply because other professors at your institution do so, and your heart is not really into teaching and supervising the preparation of such papers, consider using some other type of writing assignment in your classes. If students are not getting heartfelt, concrete guidance on a writing project, they are likely to sense that the assignment is just perfunctory, which may unintentionally encourage them to plagiarize.

If you want to avoid the research paper process altogether, you can assign in-class essays of various kinds, ranging from analyses of presentations or visuals presented in the class session to reaction papers discussing or evaluating the reading. On the other hand, because the research paper can be so valuable as a means of helping students synthesize ideas and work with information, you may want to continue requiring research, but redesign the assignments to make the process less prone to plagiarism. See Chapter 3 for ideas.

You may find it valuable to talk to your librarians about plagiarism and discover how willing they are to help you search for sources of suspect texts. Many librarians are highly supportive of faculty in this area, and their help can make a substantial difference in the effort to control the problem.

1.3.2 How seriously does your department and your university view plagiarism?

It is very difficult to fight the plagiarism battle alone, especially in the absence of a supportive administration. Talk with department colleagues and your deans to find out how seriously they view plagiarism. You may be surprised to discover that some academics view plagiarism as a sexist concept or that intellectual property smacks of capitalist imperialism, and so on. Unevenness of viewpoint and punishment will be very confusing to students.

On the other hand, if plagiarism is viewed as very serious misbehavior with strong penalties, this fact will quickly spread among students. Consider asking your college or university administration to keep statistics on how many cases of plagiarism are reported each year and how many students received each type of penalty. Dissemination of this information through the student newspaper (or other means) will indicate to students that plagiarism is taken seriously on your campus. If this information is given to student reporters for possible use in writing a story for the campus newspaper, also provide the reporters with copies of the official university policy on plagiarism, which they may choose to cite, summarize, or reproduce.

In addition to the above, you might consider suggesting that there be a single, university-wide policy on plagiarism and that the administration encourage all professors who give writing assignments to include the statement in their course outlines or syllabi. Students who see this statement in course after course (even in multiple courses during their first semester) will probably consider the risks of such misbehavior more carefully than they would without these consistently worded reminders. Syllabi might also reference the URL of an official university page offering more extensive and detailed information and rules relating to academic dishonesty.

Faculty workshops or training sessions would provide the opportunity for all faculty to understand the nature of the problem and learn what they can do to address it. You might ask your department chair, dean, or other administrator to offer training for faculty to provide education, practical tools, and the sense that the administration considers the problem a significant one.

1.3.3 Evaluate your personal feelings about plagiarism.

Plagiarism is not just a matter of kids being kids. The young people you are teaching are looking to you for guidance. Most of them expect you (sometimes unconsciously) to be a role model. If you do not take a strong stand against plagiarism, they are likely to view it as a minor matter. If you have been tempted to view plagiarism as a minor issue, to be expected from busy students, consider what students are really doing when they copy. In addition to their learning to be cynical ethical relativists, they are missing the opportunity to learn, to investigate, to think. If you do not view your assignments as providing the excitement of the chase, a feeling that the mind is alive in researching and writing, perhaps you should examine those assignments and improve them.

Chapter 2

Educating Your Students About Plagiarism

Borrowed thoughts, like borrowed money, only show the poverty of the borrower.

– Marguerite Gardiner (Lady Blessington)

As we saw in Chapter 1, ignorance and carelessness are major sources of plagiarism. Ignorance and carelessness are also major sources of excuses from students when caught plagiarizing. Even in the cases where established writers, politicians, and academics have been caught plagiarizing, the most common excuse is "confusion in my notes." The goal of this chapter is to help you educate your students about plagiarism so that they will know enough to avoid committing it willingly: They will know what it is and why they should avoid it. Regular discussions of examples and ethics throughout the term can go a long way toward inhibiting the spread of this cheating. This chapter is supported by Appendices B and C, which provide instructional materials to aid you in your teaching of the content here.

✓ 2.1 TEACH STUDENTS ABOUT PLAGIARISM.

Ideally, this instruction should begin as soon as students start writing papers using sources. It is a good idea to revisit this issue with students at the high school and college levels to ensure that the previous instruction was thorough and accurate.

2.1.1 Do not assume that students know what plagiarism is.

Even if they nod their heads when you ask them, many students may be ignorant of the difference between plagiarizing and legitimate summarizing with citation. They may even be unaware of any of the rules for quoting and paraphrasing. And, of course, a few nodding heads will not reveal what is going on in the minds of the rest of the class. Taking a few minutes to clarify matters has several benefits: It (1) educates students about the issue, (2) puts them on notice that you are strongly against cheating and will be watching, and (3) eliminates future excuses if you catch someone ("Oh, I didn't know that summarizing required a citation. I thought only copying a whole paper was plagiarism.").

Anecdote 2.1.1.1

It is interesting that students can *actually believe* that just by changing a word or two that this frees them from being guilty of plagiarism! I wonder if there are more people than we might imagine that really don't know what the word means! I had two students one time who copied most of their paper from an Internet paper service. They then each changed the structure of some of the sentences and they changed some of the vocabulary. Finally they changed the title of the paper. When I talked to them, they seemed truly shocked that I considered them to be guilty of plagiarism.

– Shirley Albertson Owens, Professor of Psychology

Anecdote 2.1.1.2

I think that students who haven't been taught about it are in a lot more danger of doing it consciously or unconsciously. I think that the problem is a lot more widespread than people think.

– Desiree Turnbow, university senior

2.1.2 Make the instruction about plagiarism as positive as possible.

Teaching students what plagiarism is should be handled as another educational task: Assume that many are in doubt or even ignorant and need the information. Similarly, warning students against the practice should be presented in as positive a way as you can manage. Remember that even in these "cheating times" the majority of students are honest. Do not treat the entire class like criminals. Give students the opportunity to thrive in an atmosphere of trust. In fact, you might rehabilitate that old Cold War slogan, "Trust, but verify." Let students know that you expect them to be honest, and that to protect the honest from the shortcutters, you will be watching carefully and penalizing appropriately.

2.1.3 Provide an explicit definition for them.

Every syllabus should have a brief but clear definition of plagiarism, and this definition should be read to the class at the first or second class meeting. (Sometimes waiting until the second or even third meeting is good because enrollment takes awhile to settle down. And the plagiarizer may just be the student who added the class late.) Below is an example taken from the author's syllabi. (Other examples in this chapter are also by the author unless specifically noted otherwise.)

Example 2.1.3.1

Plagiarism is using another person's words or ideas without giving credit to the other person. When you use someone else's words, you must put quotation marks around them and give the writer or speaker credit by revealing the source in a citation. Even if you revise or paraphrase the words of someone else or just use that person's ideas, you still must give the author credit in a note. Not giving due credit to the creator of an idea or writing is very much like lying.

See Appendix A for more examples of definitions.

2.1.4 Teach students to distinguish between plagiarism and copyright infringement.

Some students are of the opinion that if they have permission to copy a work, then they are not plagiarizing it, even though they quote it without attribution. Such students, therefore, feel free to use a roommate's paper, or text from a public domain source such as a nineteenth-century work or a government document. Your definition of plagiarism should clarify this confusion: Plagiarism is using *any words* or ideas without giving credit to the source. If the plagiarizer copies material that is also copyrighted, then the wrongdoing is potentially enhanced by the additional crime of copyright infringement.

✓ 2.2 HELP STUDENTS PREVENT UNINTENTIONAL OR INADVERTENT PLAGIARISM.

Unintentional or inadvertent plagiarism may be one of the most common sources of plagiarism. Fortunately, it can be remedied with careful instruction.

2.2.1 Show several examples of proper usage of sources and several examples of plagiarism.

In addition to a definition, you should discuss with your students the difference between appropriate, referenced use of ideas or quotations and inappropriate use. You might show them an example of a permissible paraphrase (with its citation) and an impermissible paraphrase (containing some paraphrasing and some copying), and discuss the difference. Also discuss quoting a passage and using quotation marks and a citation, as opposed to quoting a passage with neither (in other words, merely copying without attribution). Such a discussion should educate those who truly do not understand citation issues ("But I put it in my own words, so I didn't think I had to cite it") and it will also warn the truly dishonest that you are watching. See Appendix C for reproducible examples that you might use in the classroom.

"'Plagiarism?' But my roommate gave me permission to use his paper and said I didn't have to cite him."

Help students distinguish between copyright issues and plagiarism.

Anecdote 2.2.1.1

I did not really understand that I was expected to put footnotes in every report until my second year at community college. I still have some difficulty knowing when to include footnotes and how much of what I write comes from me and how much comes from the sources I have studied.... All professors, especially English professors, need to clearly explain how footnotes and bibliographies should be done and provide resources to enable students to do them correctly.

– Karla Yatckoske, university junior

2.2.2 Discuss careless note-taking techniques.

Careless note taking, where the student fails to distinguish between verbatim quotations, paraphrases, summaries, and the student's own thinking and analysis, is a source of accidental plagiarism. It is profitable to recommend that students develop a method for making such distinctions. You might give them a handout with suggestions, as in the following example:

Example 2.2.2.1

When you are making notes as you read a book or article, apply a labeling technique that will clearly distinguish what the notes represent. All word-for-word copying should be clearly placed within quotation marks. Paraphrases (turning the text into your own words) should be labeled with a mark such as a circled P. Summaries (reducing the material to a shorter form and using your own words) should be labeled with a mark such as a circled S. In all three cases, be sure to make a note of the exact page or pages the material comes from (save yourself the work of looking up the source again later). If you get an idea while reading, or want to add your own comment, interpretation, or analysis, circle that writing and attach a label such as "Mine" to it. When you return to your notes days later, you will be clear about the nature of each passage you have written down.

2.2.3 Offer a brief handout on the myths surrounding attribution.

The student culture appears to be rife with a number of myths that surround attribution and citation ("Oh, you don't have to cite that") so it might be a good idea to expose some of them. Three myths are shown in the following example:

Example 2.2.3.1

The Myths of Attribution

Myth # 1: If I mention the author's name in the text, I can copy verbatim and quotation marks are not necessary.
Fact # 1: All verbatim quotations require either quotation marks or block indentations. "Forgetting" to indent a block quotation will not be an acceptable excuse.

Myth # 2: Whatever is on the Web is not copyrighted, so it's okay to use anything there without quotation marks or attribution.
Fact # 2: This statement is doubly wrong. First, under current U.S. copyright law, everything written down is immediately copyrighted by its author. This even includes e-mail. So every Web document not explicitly labeled as being in the public domain should be considered copyrighted. Second, the copyright issue is irrelevant to the attribution question. Whenever you quote or borrow from someone else, you must cite the source. If you quote, you must use quotation marks.

Myth # 3: Since encyclopedias contain common or general knowledge, I can copy from them without attribution.
Fact # 3: While it is true that so-called common knowledge (such as the dates of birth and death of Abraham Lincoln, or the names of the fifty states) does not need attribution, quoting an encyclopedia (which may not be a very scholarly practice anyway) does require attribution and quotation marks for two reasons. First, while ideas cannot be copyrighted, the expression of ideas can be. Whenever you copy words, you must use quotation marks or block indentation for a quotation. Second, there is much more in encyclopedias than common knowledge facts. Attribution is required for any source (including encyclopedias) from which you get judgments, conclusions, viewpoints, interpretations, thoughts, ideas, evaluations, specific words or phrases, findings, controversial facts, or even interesting questions. The best rule to follow here is: When in doubt, cite it. Even if you think you have an item of common knowledge, reference its source. Overcitation is never a vice; undercitation is never a virtue.

See Appendix C for teaching materials to help students distinguish between common knowledge and information that requires citation.

✓ 2.3 DISCUSS WHY PLAGIARISM IS WRONG.

Some students may not have thought carefully about the ethical and educational reasons why plagiarism is wrong.

2.3.1 Tell students that plagiarism is unethical.

Students need to be told that plagiarism is a combination of stealing (another's words or ideas) and lying (implicitly claiming that the stolen material is the student's own). However, these facts should not be the whole emphasis of the discussion, or you risk setting up a challenge for the rebels (those who like to break the rules just for fun). Many statements on plagiarism also remind students that such cheating shows contempt for the professor, other students, and the entire academic enterprise. Plagiarizers by their actions declare that they are not at the university to gain an education, but only to pretend to do so, and that they, therefore, intend to gain by fraud the credentials (the degree) of an educated person.

The following example shows one way to represent these ideas to students during a class presentation or discussion.

Example 2.3.1.1

You may wonder why I get so upset when students plagiarize an assignment. What does plagiarism involve? First, it involves stealing someone else's intellectual property. As a published scholar, I resent this kind of theft. My reputation and in part my living depend on receiving credit for my verbal creations. To have them stolen makes me angry. Second, the plagiarizer claims that the stolen work is his or her own, thus lying to me. To lie to your professor in print shows an utter contempt for him or her, and for the entire academic enterprise. The liar is taking advantage of my respect and trust for students. If I accept the paper as legitimate, the student has committed a fraud. This counterfeit paper then competes against the papers written by honest students and perhaps puts them at a disadvantage. Thus the plagiarizer is taking advantage of (and showing no respect for) fellow students, and using me unwillingly to disadvantage them. I hope you can see why my blood boils.

Note that the following example comes from a freshman composition syllabus at a religiously affiliated private university, so that an appeal is made to Biblical principles.

Example 2.3.1.2

Plagiarism is the uncredited use of another's words *or ideas*. If you use someone else's words, you must put quotation marks around them and credit the source in a note. If you paraphrase the words of others or just use their ideas in your own words, *you still must make it clear that the ideas belong to and originate with another person and give credit in a note.* Failure to credit borrowed words or ideas is a serious breach of academic integrity. It is also a violation of the Eighth Commandment (You shall not steal) and the Ninth Commandment (You shall not bear false witness), since it involves stealing someone's words or ideas and then lying about it. Such cheating will not be tolerated. Anyone convicted of plagiarism will receive an F in the course and have a memorandum about the cheating sent to the dean of the college.

> Plagiarism is perhaps the college student's most common form of stealing.
>
> – Arthur F. Holmes

2.3.2 Consider your role in helping students evaluate their values.

The technique frequently used in "values education" is to have students engage in role playing. With respect to plagiarism, you might first describe some instances of plagiarism. For example, in one case, only one paragraph was plagiarized; in another case, the whole paper was loosely paraphrased and the student claimed not to know that wholesale paraphrasing is considered plagiarism; in a third case, the paper was simply purchased from a term paper mill and retyped to meet the instructor's formatting requirements. If you are an experienced professor, you may have some real examples to cite.

Set up a role-playing exercise and ask a student to volunteer to play you, speaking with another student who is role-playing the student who has plagiarized. Ask the student who is role-playing you to state to the other student the penalty being imposed and tell the student *why* the penalty is reasonable and justifiable. Then ask the members of the class to evaluate the role-play session in a whole-class discussion (or have them write a short paper evaluating it). Ask if they would have imposed the same penalty. Also ask if they would have given the student the same reasons for imposing it. By requiring students to consider *why* penalties are imposed, you are asking them to consider their values. See Appendix B, Section B.5, for a related activity.

2.3.3 Discuss personal integrity.

An important goal of higher education is obtaining a body of knowledge. A more important goal is the attainment of problem solving and critical thinking skills. Some would say, however, that the most important result of education is not what you learn but who you become. How does education shape the character of the student? A profitable discussion relating to the ethics of student behavior might be to ask one or more of the following questions:

➤ What kind of person hands in a downloaded paper and signs his or her name to it? When someone cheats, who is that person becoming?

➤ If your word is your bond, what is the significance of putting your name to a paper you did not write?

➤ Do you want your professors to trust you? What can you do to earn or to violate that trust? How does a breach of trust affect the entire professor-student climate?

"Here's one: 'My Apology for Cheating on the Ethics Test.' Only $19⁹⁵. That should get me off the hook."

If what you do shapes who you are, what kind of person is this?

2.3.4 Ask students to think about who is really being cheated.

Perhaps the most effective discussion will ask the students to think about who is really being cheated when someone plagiarizes. Copying papers or even parts of papers short-circuits a number of learning experiences and opportunities for the development of skills. Actually doing the work of the research paper rather than counterfeiting it gives the student not only knowledge of the subject and insights into the world of information and controversy but also improves research skills, thinking and analyzing, organizing, writing, planning and time management, and even meticulousness (those picky citation styles actually help improve one's attention to detail). All this is missed when the paper is faked, and it is these missed skills that are of high value in the working world. A degree will help students get a first job, but performance—using the skills developed by doing just such assignments as research papers—will be required not only for promotion but even for continued employment in the same position.

2.3.5 Try a thought experiment.

Here is a story you can read to your students to stimulate discussion:

A man drove his car to the repair shop for a wheel alignment. Unfortunately, the mechanic had copied and pasted his homework instead of learning the steps to use when he was taking his auto mechanic certification, so, not knowing what to do, he inadvertently made the wheels more crooked than ever. As a result, the man was in an accident and broke several bones. At the hospital, the doctor, who had cheated his way through medical school by copying other students' work, set the man's bones all wrong, leaving the man crippled and in pain. Outraged, the man decided to sue the mechanic and the doctor. He hired an attorney and went to court. Since the attorney had purchased pre-analyzed case studies in law school and turned them in as his own, he made several legal errors and the man not only lost the suit, but was successfully countersued for malicious prosecution. Sitting in his wrecked car, broke and in pain, the man thought, "Instead of copying all those term papers in college, I wish I'd done them and learned how to write. Then I could turn this experience into a great story, get it published, and pay some of my bills."

After you read this story, you might open a discussion about how plagiarism affects society (even if it does not have quite the dramatic consequences described here). Students probably expect those who serve them to have an honestly acquired education and the genuine set of skills needed to perform in a competent manner. If we cannot trust each other to be who we represent ourselves to be, how can society continue to function?

2.3.6 Discuss the Golden Rule.

The Golden Rule, "Do unto others as you would have others do unto you," is usually thought of as a part of Christian doctrine because it is expressed by Jesus in the New Testament (e.g., Matthew 7:12, Luke 6:34). However, in his book *The Words We Live By*, Brian Burrell (1997, pp. 235-40) presents expressions of the Golden Rule in eight religious traditions (Buddhism, Confucianism, Taoism, Hinduism, Jainism, Islam, Judaism, and Christianity) as well as in the writings of Isocrates and Aristotle among classical writers and in a number of modern writers ranging from Immanuel Kant to Malcom X. Therefore, discussion of this genuinely multicultural ethical principle seems legitimate in any university.

✓ 2.4 DISCUSS THE BENEFITS OF CITING SOURCES.

Discussing the benefits provided by citing sources puts a positive spin on your instruction on plagiarism.

2.4.1 Citing sources strengthens the paper.

Many students do not seem to realize that whenever they cite a source, they are strengthening their writing. Citing a source, whether paraphrased, summarized, or quoted, reveals that they have performed research work and synthesized the findings into their own argument. Using sources shows that the student is engaged in "the great conversation," the world of ideas, and that the student is aware of other thinkers' positions on the topic. By quoting (and citing) writers who support the student's position, the student adds strength to the position. By responding reasonably to those who oppose the position, the student shows that there are valid counter arguments. In a nutshell, citing helps make the essay stronger and sounder and will probably result in a better grade.

2.4.2 Citing sources shows respect for intellectual property.

Appropriate quoting and citing also evidences the student's respect for the creators of ideas and arguments—honoring thinkers and their intellectual property. Most college graduates will become knowledge workers themselves, earning at least part of their living creating information products. They therefore have an interest in maintaining a respect for intellectual property and the proper attribution of ideas and words.

2.4.3 Citing is a service to the reader.

The "official" reason for citing sources is not merely to give due credit but to enable the reader to locate the sources and pursue further reading or investigation about that aspect of the topic. A brief quotation or reference may have stimulated an interest the reader can satisfy by finding the source and reading the entire account, or the writer may have raised questions or doubts the reader wants to satisfy. "How can Jones say that?" can be answered only if the reader can go to Jones and find out—by reading the full context, seeing Jones's own sources, and so on.

In the case of academic essays, where the writing process is one of learning how to think and analyze, the professor may suspect that the student has misinterpreted or misunderstood an author's central idea, and the actual case can be determined only by a look at the source.

✓ 2.5. DISCUSS SOME OF YOUR DETECTION WORK.

Not as a means of throwing down the gauntlet of challenge, but as a friendly putting on notice, you might want to tell students about some of your experiences and techniques relating to plagiarism. Honest students will love your stories and feel secure that you are watching out for academic integrity. Those still confused about what is and is not acceptable will gain further insight. And those who will do anything they can get away with will—it is to be hoped—have second thoughts.

2.5.1 Tell war stories.

Remember the student who handed in a chapter from the recommended reading, or the one who presented you with a letter-perfect "draft," or the paper with someone else's name whited out? Tell your students about your own experiences catching plagiarists, and mention in passing the penalties they suffered. Try not to gloat or sneer; just let them know you are watching and catching. If you have a few particularly clever or challenging success stories to tell, include those, so that students will realize that it is not just lack of cleverness that gets cheaters caught.

2.5.2 Take them to or mention paper mill sites.

If you have classroom data projection capability, take your students to any one of the dozens of sites listed in Appendix E and look around. Show them a paper or two from the free sites and comment on how poorly written they are. If you do not have projection capability, you can still make overhead transparencies of a paper and mention that you visit these sites, looking for papers occasionally. If you take them to some of the commercial sites, include some value analysis in your commentary.

Here is an example of what might be said as a commentary to accompany a look at one such free essay found on-line:

Example 2.5.2.1

More than a dozen free paper sites offer a particular essay on Jonathan Swift's *Gulliver's Travels*. Quite aside from the fact that it is poorly written and contains many errors of spelling and punctuation, the essay contains a veritable cornucopia of preposterous anachronisms and factual errors that anyone who had read the novel even cursorily would immediately recognize. Imagine an English professor reading that in this novel written in 1726, one of the characters says he has read nineteenth-century author Charles Dickens. The reader of this paper also learns that the Houyhnhnms walk on two legs and play the flute (which they do not) and that Queen Elizabeth had a husband (which she did not). It can only be wondered whether this paper is some kind of Trojan horse (to borrow a concept from the arena of software viruses) designed to ruin students who submit downloaded papers. And one must wonder how many other such papers like it are in those free essay databases.

Here is a sample commentary that might accompany a look at a listing for a paper on a fee-based paper mill site:

Example 2.5.2.2

Oh, look. Here you can get a 10-page paper on acid rain for only $89.50. And all you lose is the benefit of learning something, improving yourself, your integrity and self-respect, and, in this case, possibly a passing grade because you can't determine the quality of the paper from the listing.

"Here's one that's been bought so many times it's *fifty percent off now.* It's called, 'Radical Individualism: I Speak for Myself.'"

2.5.3 Mention some of your resources.

Students are quite aware that the Web and electronic databases have opened up wide opportunities for them to "download their workload" as the cheating sites say, but they may be less aware that the strategies and tools of detection are also proliferating. It might be valuable for you to mention just a few of your tools and techniques. You might say that you use a combination of internal evidence (the "clues" mentioned in the first section of Chapter 4) and external evidence (the source documents themselves). You might even use this book as a "show and tell" in class to let students know you are up on the subject. Even a comment such as, "You know, professors know how to do research, too," might help.

✓ 2.6 MAKE THE PENALTIES CLEAR.

Students should be made aware of the penalties for plagiarism as early as possible.

2.6.1 Quote institutional policy.

If an institutional policy exists, quote it in your syllabus. If you have your own policy, specify the penalties involved. For example, "Cheating on a paper will result in an F on that paper with no possibility of a makeup. A second act of cheating will result in an F in the course regardless of the student's grade otherwise." If you teach at a university where the penalty for plagiarism is dismissal from the university or being reported to the academic dean or dean of students, you should make that clear as well.

2.6.2 State your own policy and feelings.

If you feel strongly about plagiarism, consider warning students about your *feelings* (not just university or departmental policies) in your syllabus. One of the contributors to this book presents the statement shown in Example 2.6.2.1 in his syllabus. While the statement might be viewed as rather egotistical and harsh, the professor should be given credit for being up front with his students. You might consider writing a *personal* statement regarding *your feelings* about plagiarism and including it in your syllabus. As an added benefit, following this guideline will give students some insight into your personal values. Sharing your personal values (as long as they do not cross the boundaries of the separation of state and church in publicly supported colleges and universities) is, of course, an important component of values education.

If your personal feelings are especially strong, it is a good idea to pass your statement by an appropriate administrator for feedback prior to incorporating it in your syllabi. Such a check does not in any way preclude the presentation of a robust declaration, as the following example shows:

Example 2.6.2.1

Important Notice: I have a Ph.D. in Educational Research from a first-rate university. I was privileged to attend the university and am very proud of the scholarly contributions I have been able to make to the academy of scholars as a result of my education. I am willing to do my best to provide you with the same quality of instruction that I received. If you work diligently and keep in close contact with me regarding class assignments, I believe that you will learn many interesting facts, principles, theories, and inquiry skills. With a reasonable amount of effort, you should be able to earn a good grade even in this highly technical course. However, you should be forewarned that I have no tolerance for the following: (1) plagiarism (see the definition below), (2) cheating while taking examinations, and (3) failure to do homework. I take any of these behaviors as a personal affront and a *personal insult*. If you engage in any of these behaviors, it will consume my time by forcing me to keep logs of your behavior, holding conferences with you, filing grievances against you, meeting with the University's Grievance Officer regarding your behavior, and so on. In more than 30 years of teaching, I have found that about one in 50 students fails to pay proper attention to this notice. To the vast majority of you, I apologize for sounding condescending because I am fully aware that almost all of you are here to work hard, be honest, learn, and make a contribution to society through your role as educators. This notice is included in this syllabus for the few who dare to personally insult me. There are multiple sections of this course, each taught by a different instructor. Those who find my personal dislikes described above unappealing should bring me a drop slip, which I will gladly sign.

– Anonymous, Professor of Education

2.6.3 Present penalties in a positive way.

Even the penalties can be presented in a positive light. Penalties exist to reassure honest students that their efforts are respected and valued, so much so that those who would escape the work by fakery will be punished substantially. (Honest students feel highly encouraged by clearly stated cheating penalties.)

The following examples provide possible ways of describing the penalties:

Example 2.6.3.1

In order to guarantee the value of doing your own work, students who do not do their own work—those who copy from another person or who plagiarize their papers—will be given an F in the course.

Example 2.6.3.2

Honesty is so highly prized in this course that any attempt to counterfeit it through plagiarism or cheating will be punished by a zero on the assignment and possibly a failing grade in the course.

This chapter closes with two comments from honest students eager to see plagiarizers caught:

Anecdote 2.6.3.1

I am rather disappointed, however, at how little some profs care [about plagiarism]. It is a known fact that *many* students plagiarize. It is also a known fact that *many* students get away with plagiarism.

– Andrew Yeager, university freshman

Anecdote 2.6.3.2

I really don't like it when people copy homework or cheat on tests because I feel like they cheat me because I work harder for my grades than they do. It is also unfair when the class grades are set on a curve and the cheaters help push the curve up and make it harder for the rest of the class that is actually trying. I think that taking a closer look at homework and enforcing the penalties would greatly decrease the cheating in schools.

– Anonymous, university freshman

Chapter 3

Constructing Assignments to Prevent Plagiarism

Most plagiarists, like the drone, have not the taste to select, the industry to acquire, nor the skills to improve, but
imprudently pilfer the honey ready from the hive.

– Charles Caleb Colton

An ounce of prevention is worth a pound of cure.

– Proverb

In problem-solving theory, the so-called "stop it" solutions
that eliminate or prevent the problem are considered superior to the
"mop it" solutions that merely deal with the consequences of a
problem. So, too, in combating plagiarism, methods of prevention
should receive major emphasis. Detection and punishment are
challenging and time consuming, and there will likely always be
cases that end with a lack of sufficient proof. On the other hand,
prevention measures, if carefully applied, hold the hope for substantially reducing plagiarism in the first place. The overall goal of
the specific strategies in this chapter is to make research assignments and requirements unique enough that an off-the-shelf paper
or a paper written for another class or a friend's paper—or even a

quick cut-and-paste job—will not fulfill the requirements. Only a newly written paper will.

✓ 3.1 MAKE THE ASSIGNMENT CLEAR.

The clearer and more specific you make a research paper assignment, the less likely a student will be able to find an off-the-shelf paper that matches it. Clarity helps students understand what is expected of them and encourages them to do their own work because they feel more confident about exactly what to do.

3.1.1 Be specific about your expectations.

Should the paper be an individual effort, or is collaboration permitted? Must the paper be unique to your course, or do you allow it to be submitted to another course as well? (In scholarly publishing, such multiple publication is usually called self-plagiarism. If you require a unique paper, be sure to prohibit photocopied papers and insist on original typescripts or printouts.) What kind of research do you require? How should it be evidenced in the paper, by quotation or just summary? It has been claimed that a major source of poor student papers (not just plagiarizing) is the unclear assignment. You might ask another faculty member to read your paper assignment and discuss with you whether or not it is clear and detailed enough for students to fulfill in the way you intend.

3.1.2 Consider requiring all students in the course to write on the same topic.

While this idea may be less desirable in a freshman composition class in which students have a variety of majors and widely divergent interests, it might be considered in upper-division content classes in which all students have the same major. In a social psychology class, for example, you might require all students to write a research paper on road rage, with an emphasis on psychological theories that help to explain it. You might even encourage students to share their references with one another (with the proviso that a student should not share references with another student who has no references to share in return). This provides the benefit of encouraging students to share and discuss information with one another (as scholars tend to do) while discouraging them from plagiarizing because others in the class are expecting them to participate in sharing references. Of course, you can require students to write their individual papers in their own individual styles, reflecting their personal perspectives on the issue. The variations in research and personal approach should keep the assignment from becoming overly boring to you.

An additional benefit of following this guideline is that after reading multiple papers on the same topic, you will become somewhat of an expert on it. Note that it is easier for an expert to spot a plagiarized paper than someone who has only passing knowledge of a topic.

If you follow this guideline, expect some students to complain that they want to write a paper on a topic of burning interest to them. Point out to such students that the purpose of the assignment is to teach them skills they can use to investigate any problem of interest to them in the future. Help them understand that the mastery of inquiry and communication skills is a more important aim of a college education than the acquisition of knowledge on a particular topic. Furthermore, it is important for knowledge workers to develop the ability to make any subject interesting—to themselves and to others—since they will not always be able to choose the information they are required to work with on the job.

3.1.3 Consider providing a list of highly specific topics.

Another approach to the assignment of topics is to develop a collection of topics related to the course material and require students to choose from among them. Change topics from semester to semester whenever possible. Unusual topics or topics with a narrow twist are good because there will be fewer papers already written on them. If you provide a substantial enough list of topics (say two dozen), most students will find something that can interest them. You can also allow for a custom topic if the student comes to discuss it with you first.

Example 3.1.3.1

Instead of "Treatment of Schizophrenia," use "Efficacy of New Psychotropic Medications for Schizophrenia."

Example 3.1.3.2

Instead of "The Globalization of the Fast Food Industry," use "KFC Goes to China: A Lesson in International Fast-Food Marketing."

3.1.4 Have students narrow their chosen topics.

If you allow students to choose their own topics, invite them to your office for a topic conference, where you help them focus and customize their topics. The topics of many downloaded or purchased research papers are often quite general, so by narrowing, you can inhibit the use of prewritten papers.

Here are two examples of papers available for downloading. Notice that both are quite general. To prevent submission of general papers of this type, suggest revisions to narrow the topics when students offer to write papers on broad topics.

Example 3.1.4.1

Paper available for sale from Term-Papers-on-File.com:
Topic:
"Affirmative Action / Do We Really Need It?"
On-line description:
A 16-page exploration of three decades of Affirmative Action policies. Includes the pros and cons of Affirmative Action and an examination of current public sentiment toward these policies. Bibliography lists several sources.

Narrow topics for which it would be more difficult to find an on-line paper:

"Recent Legal Developments Affecting Affirmative Action," or "Psychological Research on the Effects of Affirmative Action," or "Recent State Legislature Battles over Affirmative Action."

"I have a paper here, 'American Wilderness: Challenge or Threat,' but I don't know who wrote it. If any of you knows, please inform me. And that includes all four of you who turned it in."

Example 3.1.4.2

Paper available for sale from Term-Papers-on-File.com:
Topic:
"Salesmanship on the Internet"
On-line description:
A 10-page essay discussing using the Internet as a sales tool. Electronic selling is very different than other kinds of media and the businessperson needs to consider numerous issues, such as the type of consumer that uses the Internet to make purchases. Many different aspects are discussed, including sales strategies, populations of consumers, tips for getting started, types of Internet resources one can use and more.
Narrow topics for which it would be more difficult to find an on-line paper:
"Selling Books on the Internet: A Brief History," or "The Success of Auction Sites on the Internet," or "Customer Resource Management in the On-line Store."

3.1.5 Consider prohibiting students from uploading papers to paper mills.

A number of "free" paper sites actually employ a bartering system. The typical arrangement requires a student first to upload a research paper that he or she previously wrote (or somehow acquired), in order to gain access to the site to download other papers. The papers that students upload in order to gain access to the site become available to other students.

Some free paper sites have recently posted a notice to faculty members to the effect that a student should not be accused of plagiarism simply because the faculty member has found the paper on the paper site. The student may be innocent, these sites explain, because it is the student's own paper that has been uploaded to the site, rather than a downloaded paper that has been turned in by the student. Such a claim, of course, appears to have about the same credibility as the disclaimer that "these papers are for research purposes only." Nevertheless, as a means of avoiding any such excuses, you might want to include as part of the paper assignment an explicit prohibition against the uploading (or otherwise sharing) of the paper. You should also warn students to guard their papers and computer files carefully, because another student may upload a borrowed or stolen paper (at a site that requires a trade, for example), thereby exposing the actual writer to a charge of plagiarism. Students should be cautioned to save all their notes and drafts and to inform the professor immediately if they suspect a paper has been stolen.

✓ 3.2 BREAK THE ASSIGNMENT INTO PIECES.

The temptation to plagiarize can be strong for the procrastinating student who sees only that a research paper is due at the end of the course. Nothing may get done until the last minute, when the student suddenly gives in and borrows a friend's paper or downloads one from the Web. This event can be largely obviated by requiring multiple due dates for sections of the paper in progress and by asking for custom components in the paper.

3.2.1 Require specific components of the paper.

Papers that are downloaded or copied from others are essentially "as found" objects—their components are fixed. Adding components to such papers often proves difficult for plagiarists, who are unfamiliar with the background and research behind the paper. And such students may be too hurried to want to add items piecemeal. Here are some examples of specific requirements:

Example 3.2.1.1

"The paper must make use of two Internet sources, two printed book sources, two printed journal sources, one personal interview, and one personally conducted survey." Notice that this kind of recipe requirement will be difficult to match off the shelf, yet it maintains a wide degree of freedom for the student in selecting specific sources. This example also shows how you can assure that the student will use a variety of research materials and not rely solely on the Web or on articles. This kind of breadth requirement, therefore, has several benefits.

Example 3.2.1.2

"You must make use of Wells's article on 'Intelligent Design Principles,' and some material from either the Jones or Smith book." Here, a specific book or article is required as a source for the paper. The requirement could be different for each student (where you choose an article or two that seems to fit with the particular topic or research problem), or you could have everyone use the same source or sources, depending on the nature of the assignment. Building in a few specific sources at the beginning of a research project is much easier than trying to stuff some references into a preexistent paper. The articles could be available on-line (from the Web or one of your university's proprietary databases) to save the effort of photocopying and distribution.

Example 3.2.1.3

"Include a graph that represents the data discussed in the first section, and present the data in tabular format as well." Most of the old papers lack any kind of graphics, so requiring some electronically inserted graphics in a paper not only helps deter mindless copying but also will help students learn the skills necessary to complete such a requirement. In addition, students may begin to see how illustrations can enhance a presentation.

Example 3.2.1.4

"At least three of your twelve sources (minimum) must have been published or written within the past year." A requirement like this will quickly outdate most paper mill products.

Example 3.2.1.5

"In the analysis section, you should discuss your interpretation of data set B, which has been distributed to you." As with requiring a specific book or article, incorporating some information you provide will cause the student to do some fresh work with the information, again inhibiting the temptation to grab a prewritten paper from somewhere else.

Example 3.2.1.6

"The paper must include a personal interview with an expert or authority." An interview creates both a current and a checkable source. It also has the benefits of currency, variety of research type (students realize that not all sources of information are published books or articles), and the stimulation of interest (some students find doing interviews very engaging).

Example 3.2.1.7

"The paper should include examples drawn from your own personal experience, such as your part-time employment, athletic activities, community service, or travel experience."

Example 3.2.1.8

"Be sure you include a response to the ideas developed in the class discussions of the previous two weeks. What is a workable way to meet the challenges raised?"

If a student does begin with someone else's paper and has to work additional material such as the above into it, you will probably be able to tell. For example, the writing styles will differ, or the fit will be awkward where the new material has been inserted.

3.2.2 Require process steps for the paper.

Set a series of due dates throughout the term for the various steps of the research paper process: topic or problem, preliminary bibliography, prospectus, research material (annotated photocopies of articles, for example), outline, rough draft, final annotated bibliography, final draft. Some of these parts can be reverse-engineered by the determined cheater, but most students should realize that doing the assignment honestly is easier than the alternative.

If you have a large class and can require only a few of these steps because of simple logistics and workload, at least require a rough draft. The rough draft serves several functions. A quick glance will reveal whether whole sections are appearing without citations. At the draft stage, you have the opportunity to educate the student further and discuss how proper citation works. You can also mark places and ask for more research material to be incorporated. If you are suspicious of the paper at this point, ask for the incorporation of some specific material that you name, such as a particular book or article. (See some other possibilities described above.) Keep the drafts and let students know that you expect major revisions and improvements between drafts. Requiring a rough draft is also an excellent means of improving students' writing, quite apart from the other goal of preventing plagiarism, because it encourages them to revisit and revise their material.

3.2.3 Divide the total credit for the assignment among the parts.

Instead of just checking off the outline or note cards or rough draft, assign a number of points to each component. If a student fails to turn in several parts, the final grade on the assignment will reflect that.

Example 3.2.3.1

The research paper is worth 200 points, divided as follows: topic, 10; preliminary bibliography, 10; prospectus, 20; notes and outline, 10; rough draft, 50; final draft, 100.

Note in Example 3.2.3.1 that the final version of the paper is worth one-half the total points for the assignment. Other components that are poorly done or missing will have a substantial effect on the final grade. This point-spreading method also has the benefit of encouraging students to work through the research and drafting process. Even if you decide not to require all these components, you could still require a draft and assign points to it (perhaps one-third to one-half the total points). By making suggestions on the draft and expecting substantial revision, you will help prevent the receipt of canned papers.

"*This paper is right on!* I sure wish I'd written it. *Hmm...maybe I will!*"

3.2.4 Have students include an annotated bibliography.

The annotation should include a brief summary of the source, where it was located (including the call number for books or complete URL for Web or other Internet sources), and an evaluation about the usefulness of the source. (Optionally, as a lesson in information quality, ask students to comment on why they thought the source was credible.) The normal process of research makes completing this task easy, but it creates headaches for students who have copied a paper from someone else since few papers include annotated bibliographies like this. Another benefit of this assignment is that students must reflect on the reliability and quality of their sources.

Example 3.2.4.1

"The Annotated List of Works Cited should list only works actually referred to in the paper, and should follow MLA bibliographic style. Each entry must be accompanied by a six- to eight-line annotation that describes and evaluates the work. As appropriate, address some of these questions: How useful was the work? What did it cover? Was it up-to-date? What audience was it written for? Why did you judge it to be credible?"

3.2.5 Require most references to be up-to-date.

Many of the free term papers on-line (and many of the ones for sale) are quite old, with correspondingly old references. If you require all research material to be, say, less than five years old, you will automatically eliminate thousands of on-line papers. Such a recent date restriction is not usually workable for some subjects, such as history or English literature, but you can always require a few sources of recent date.

Example 3.2.5.1

"Of the minimum of eight sources for the paper, at least two must have been written or published within the last five years."

Example 3.2.5.2

"For your trend analysis, you must use statistics (births, deaths, marriages, divorces) that include last year's numbers. A current almanac or Web site will supply these."

Anecdote 3.2.5.1

When I assign a major paper, I require sources from business journals dated during the semester. At least the students can't just copy a last-semester student's paper.

– Rob Nelson, Professor of Business

3.2.6 Require photocopies or printouts of sources.

Either as a separate component in the process or with the final paper, you can require students to turn in copies of their source articles, either photocopied from print journals or printed from the Web or an electronic database. For book sources, you can require photocopies of the page or pages referred to in the citation. You might also make it clear that you expect these sources to be marked with highlighter, pen, or pencil to demonstrate that they have been thoroughly read and interacted with. The printouts will (1) serve as a deterrent to copying, (2) provide you with comparison text to see how accurately students quote, paraphrase, summarize, and cite, and (3) save you the trouble of hunting up sources and Web sites yourself in cases of suspected plagiarizing, whether inadvertent or deliberate.

Requiring copies of sources is one of the most powerful deterrents to plagiarism and should receive serious consideration. Imagine the difficulty for a student who downloads a paper: trying to locate all of the sources (which may not even be possible), printing them off or photocopying them, marking them up, and hunting the passages cited in the paper. Even a plagiarizer would learn a lot about the research process.

3.2.7 Do not allow students to change topics at the last minute.

Sometimes a student will go through the process of supplying a topic and perhaps even a prospectus, only to come to you a week before the paper is due and ask to change the topic. Often the argument is that there is not sufficient research material to complete the paper. (If you require a bibliography early in the process, this argument should be unavailable.) This request is, of course, a major red flag, and may indicate that the student is planning to use a shrink-wrapped product. Some language in the syllabus or in class prohibiting changing after a certain date might be appropriate.

✓ 3.3 REQUIRE INTERACTION AND FEEDBACK.

For the best learning to take place, the paper-writing process should not be considered over once the student hands the paper in. Asking students to think about and discuss their own work and to react to the work of other students will give them a sense that they have engaged not merely in the completion of a project but in the creation of knowledge worthy of sharing. Knowing in advance that this activity is part of the assignment will also encourage them to write the paper and learn about the subject.

3.3.1 Consider having each student obtain written feedback from at least two other students.

Freshman composition classes use this "peer editing" or "quality circle" technique quite commonly. It can be even more effective in upper division classes, where majors are familiar with the subject matter and citation style of the discipline.

To implement it in its simplest form, you can require each student to have his or her paper read by at least two other students for feedback. You can require these other students to write a brief statement on what suggestions they made for improving the paper. Each student should be required to staple these statements at the end of his or her research paper. Students can also be required to write a brief statement indicating which suggestions they took from other students in revising their papers as well as why some, if any, suggestions were rejected.

A more complex implementation of this guideline would require written feedback from other students at each stage of the writing process such as topic selection, writing the initial outline, and so on.

In addition to discouraging plagiarism, this guideline has the added benefit of encouraging students to interact with each other in a scholarly way.

3.3.2 Require oral reports of student papers.

Ask students questions about their research and writing process. If students know at the beginning of the term that they will be giving a presentation on their research papers to the rest of the class, they will recognize the need to be very familiar with both the process and the content of the paper. Such knowledge should serve as a strong deterrent against simply copying a paper. Regardless of how many times a student rereads a copied paper, much of the knowledge of the research, the drafting and revising, what had to be left out, and so on will still remain unknown. Alternative to an in-class presentation is a one-on-one office meeting, where you can quiz the student about several aspects of the paper as needed.

Example 3.3.2.1

"When I finish reading your paper, I will return it to you individually at an office conference, where I will ask you a few questions about your research and writing process and why you took the direction you did with the argument. So be sure you make a few notes about these details as you research and construct the paper." This kind of "on notice" language should seem a matter of course for honest students and will be a warning to students tempted to look for short cuts.

Anecdote 3.3.2.1

When I require book reviews, I require a 20–30 minute oral review as well as the written one. Failure to have done the actual work shows up immediately during an oral report, and especially during the questions afterward.

– Rob Nelson, Professor of Business

3.3.3 Require a metalearning essay.

On the day you collect the papers, have students write an in-class essay about what they learned from the assignment. What problems did they face and how did they overcome them? What research strategy did they follow? Where did they locate most of their sources? What is the most important thing they learned from investigating this subject?

Example 3.3.3.1

"For the next ten minutes, write an essay of at least a good paragraph or two describing how you researched the paper. Did you begin at the library, on the Web, with reference books, talking with others, or what? How did you proceed after that? Describe the problems or blind alleys you encountered along the way. What proved to be your most fruitful research technique?"

"But you can't give me a *B-minus* on this paper! The girl who actually *wrote* it got an 'A' from her professor just last semester!"

Example 3.3.3.2

"Write a paragraph or two describing what you learned from researching and writing this paper. You can focus either on what you learned about the process of constructing the paper (problem framing, researching, thinking, writing, editing) or what you learned about the subject itself (the major areas of controversy, historical progress, current approaches, and so on)."

For most students who actually did the research paper, this assignment will help them think about their own learning. It also provides you with information about the students' knowledge of their papers and gives you a writing sample to compare with the papers. If a student's knowledge of the paper and its process seems modest or if the in-class essay quality diverges strikingly from the writing ability shown in the paper, further investigation is probably warranted.

3.3.4 Require an integrity statement.

When students hand in their papers, have them attach a signed statement to the effect that they are the true author of the paper. The paper is not acceptable without the signed statement. If you use such a declaration, show it to students before they begin the research process so they will be aware of the required attestation well in advance. The following three examples illustrate how such a statement might be worded:

Example 3.3.4.1
Writer's Declaration:
I certify that I am the true author of this entire paper, except where quotations or paraphrases are clearly indicated and cited, and that I have made every effort to produce the best paper I can. I have edited and proofread carefully, and I take full responsibility for the quality of this product.

Example 3.3.4.2

By my signature below I hereby declare that

1. I have written this paper myself and have not obtained it in whole or in part from another source;
2. I have used quotation marks or block indentations for all words quoted verbatim; and
3. I have included citations for all borrowed ideas, whether quoted, paraphrased, summarized, or referred to in passing.

If you write a statement based on the following example, be certain that you clearly prohibit disk and paper lending in your syllabus (and mention this in class) so students will not be caught with a self-written paper but unable to sign this statement.

Example 3.3.4.3

I hereby affirm that (1) the research and writing of this paper are entirely my own; (2) I have not intentionally plagiarized any portion of this paper but have used quotation marks and citations appropriately; and (3) I have not helped any other student inappropriately by lending my notes, paper, disk, files, or other materials.

3.3.5 Appeal to the honor code.

If your institution has an honor code, discuss it and its implications in class. Refer to it in your syllabus in the cheating and plagiarism note. If your institution does not have an honor code, consider lobbying for one. See Chapter 6 for more information and Appendix A, Section A.3, for sample honor code language.

Chapter 4

Strategies for Detecting Plagiarism

In comparing various authors with one another, I have discovered that some of the gravest and latest writers have transcribed, word for word, from former works, without making acknowledgement.

> – Pliny the Elder,
> *Historia Naturalis*

Yet literary plagiarism is possibly unique among crimes. It's robbery...but unlike most forms of robbery, the thief puts what he's stolen on open display. . . . He makes a museum display of it and invites people in. For that's what it's about: to take all the credit for what's on show (which is why the matter of whether the source is acknowledged or not is crucial). And unusually in crimes, the crime will be preserved indefinitely.

> – Richard Rush

Though you may educate your students thoroughly and plan assignments that preclude the possibility of wholesale plagiarism (turning in a prepackaged mill paper, for example), there will still be the likelihood of at least occasional copy-and-paste performances. This chapter therefore covers the standard clues that identify copying (for the benefit of those new to grading student research papers) and some more subtle indicators that experienced graders might find valuable. Information on term paper mills and on searching electronic databases and the Internet is included, together with a list and discussion of commercial detection software and services.

The concept of "detection" ranges from mere "red flag" suspicion to overwhelming and probably irrefutable evidence. Before evidence can be adduced, some suspicion about the work must be aroused. The suspicion invites further investigation. The clues described in the first two sections are the red flags; the searching methods in the latter half of the chapter are to help prove or disprove the suspicion.

✓ 4.1 LOOK FOR OBVIOUS CLUES.

Many student plagiarists are amateur cheaters who lack the sophistication or cunning to hide their tracks. As a result, you will often find the cheating betrayed by some rather obvious indicators. As you read the papers, look for internal evidence that may indicate plagiarism. Among the clues are the following:

4.1.1 Mixed citation or bibliographic styles.

If some paragraphs are cited in MLA style, while other references are in APA, and perhaps one or two are in CBE or Chicago, you are probably looking at a paste-up. Similarly, even if the in-text citation is consistent and appropriate to the style you assigned, check the bibliography for variation. Inaccuracy in one style reflects inadequate learning or carefulness, but mixed styles may reflect mixed copying.

4.1.2 Lack of citations or quotations.

Lengthy, well-written sections without documentation may have been taken from general knowledge sources, such as encyclopedias, popular magazines, or Web sites. Papers with too few references may also be cause for investigation, especially if you have assigned a larger number. A number of the free papers on the Web feature only three or four references.

4.1.3 Dead-end internal references.

If you are reading along and the text says, "See Table 2" and there is no Table 2, perhaps Table 2 was not copied along with the rest of the text. Or if the in-text citation refers to Maximilian, and there is no such entry in the bibliography, either the student has botched the reference or the passage has been copied.

4.1.4 Unusual formatting.

Strange or inconsistent margins, skewed tables, lines broken in half, mixed subhead styles and other formatting anomalies may indicate a hasty copy and paste job. Sometimes an on-line source will have line feeds without carriage returns, so that when copied and pasted, there will be a short line of text with the next line picking up right below it rather than beginning at the left margin.

4.1.5 Off topic.

If the paper does not develop one of the assigned topics or even the topic it announces, it may have been borrowed at the last minute or downloaded. Similarly, if parts of the paper do develop the subject, but other parts seem oddly off, the paper may be a cut-and-paste product. Students will occasionally take a packaged paper and try to write it into the topic by adding sentences or paragraphs here and there. However, the other paragraphs clearly discuss something else.

4.1.6 Logical inconsistency.

Copy-and-paste papers often reveal a glaring lack of seamlessness in the flow and logic of the argument. For example, if you are reading a paper purportedly about pesticide residues and you find mention in a paragraph something about "the economic importance of further innovation of these systems," or some such language that does not match the subject, you are likely reading pieces from two or more sources. Another example might be references to "our experiment" in a paper by a single author who elsewhere never mentions an experiment.

4.1.7 Signs of datedness.

If there are no references after some well past date (e.g., 1985), or if a data table offers a company's sales from, say, 1989 to 1994, either the student is using very old material or the paper itself is rather old.

4.1.8 Dead URLs in citations.

The Web is an ever-changing place, and pages are moved or removed regularly, resulting in that not uncommon "Error 404: Page Not Found" or similar message. However, if a paper with several Web sources has more than one or two dead links, that may be an indication that substantial time has passed since the paper was written. In the course of a single term, not more than a link or two should normally be expected to expire. (Of course, you may also have a student who is typing in rather than pasting in the URLs and making typing errors. As part of your assignment of the paper, you might require students to double-check their URLs before handing in the paper.)

4.1.9 Anachronisms.

If the paper refers to long-past events as current ("Only after the Gulf War is over will we see lower oil prices" or "Why isn't the Carter administration acting on this?"), you almost certainly have a recycled paper on your hands. Look also for the less obvious anachronisms, such as implying an event is still in the future when it has now passed ("Netscape will soon face competition from Microsoft in the Web browser business").

4.1.10 Familiarity.

Stories abound about professors who have found themselves reading remarkably familiar text in a student paper, only to discover that the paper had been copied from some source known to the professor. Last year's textbook, last semester's papers, even the professor's own published work—all have been reported to be sources of copying.

Anecdote 4.1.10.1

Several years ago I was teaching a section of Introduction to Business. As one of the course requirements, the students all had to write term papers. While grading the papers I found two identical papers, but each with a different student's name on it. After confronting the two students I learned that each of them had purchased the paper from a student at [a nearby university], and neither of the students knew the other had purchased the paper. Obviously, neither student passed. You can draw whatever conclusions you wish regarding the seller and the buyers, and I have probably already had the same thoughts.

– Rob Nelson, Professor of Business

Anecdote 4.1.10.2

What I observed, over the years, is that close friends or students in study groups often tend to have similarly written papers. I always compare "kinship" related papers.

– Shirley Albertson Owens, Professor of Psychology

"How did you like my research paper?"

"I like it better every year."

4.1.11 Smoking guns.

This category might be called "blunders of the clueless" since it includes obvious indicators of copying. Reported in the past have been labels left at the end of papers ("Thank you for using Term-PaperMania"), title pages stapled to Web printouts (complete with date and URL in the corners), title pages claiming the paper is by

Tom Jones when subsequent pages say "Smith, page 2," and papers with whiteout over the previous author's name. A paper will occasionally make an institutionally specific reference, which is clearly not to your institution. "Professor Carlson, who teaches history here at the university," in a paper at a school that has no Professor Carlson, is a giveaway. (There is another example below, in Anecdote 4.2.1.1, where a student at a semester-system college referred to the school as being on the quarter system.)

Few of these clues will provide courtroom proof of plagiarism, of course, but their presence should alert you to investigate the paper further. Even if you do not find the source of the paper, you may be able to use these clues profitably in a discussion with the student in your office. See Chapter 5 for some ideas about such discussions.

✓ 4.2 LOOK FOR THE MORE SUBTLE CLUES.

Even students who are clever enough to avoid the more obvious indicators of plagiarized work often cannot avoid the more subtle clues without rewriting the entire paper. A writing thief may doctor the citations to assure that they are all consistent with the assigned style, but may lack the time, knowledge, or expertise to doctor the larger discrepancies.

4.2.1 Anomalies of style.

Many seasoned faculty first lift an eyebrow of suspicion over a paper because of a subtle odor of theft arising from some almost indefinable incongruity of the writing style. Either the style changes from section to section, or it is too sophisticated for the level of the student, or it is not quite current in expression. Attention to the style, then, can be an important clue.

Is the writing style odd or unusual in any way that cannot be explained easily (that is, by the fact that the student is a non-native speaker of English or that the topic itself involves abstract complexity)? For example, are there two-page paragraphs that remind you of a nineteenth-century encyclopedia? Is there ornate rhetorical structure? Are there many more metaphors than you would usually expect? Does the introduction get in its own way and stumble around, only to give way to glowing, flowing discourse? Is there a mixture of British and American punctuation or spelling, with consistent usage within large sections? (For example, do some sections discuss the "flavouring" of the company's product while other sections discuss its "flavoring"?) An in-class essay is a good way to obtain a sample of the student's prose so that you can discover whether rhetorical or stylistic flourishes are actually native to the student.

Anecdote 4.2.1.1

One of the most obvious cases of plagiarism I dealt with involved a second-semester senior who submitted a term paper for an upper-division course in ethics. The disjointed cut-and-paste writing style between the introduction and the body of the paper was the first clue that it appeared that one person wrote the intro and another person wrote the body, and then "the author" returned back to the original style for the concluding summary. My uneasiness was confirmed when I read a footnote that referred to…[our college's] "quarter system." Since we were on a semester system, I knew that something was awry. There were other allusions in the footnote to this institution on the "quarter system" that didn't fit the college's profile. So, I made an appointment with the student…. The student confessed that he got the paper from a friend at a seminary in the area and under the pressure of time used it as his own. He did redo the paper and passed the course. He later told me that my confrontation of his plagiarism was one of the most important experiences he had at the college. He learned the importance of honesty and truth telling in a way that internalized the ethics textbook used in the course.

— Murray Dempster, Professor of Social Ethics

4.2.2 Anomalies of diction.

Many undergraduates do not understand the concept of levels of diction. They think all words are equally welcome in every paper. As a result, when those who plagiarize with the cut-and-paste method perform their deeds, they often mix paragraphs of varying levels together—the sophisticated scholar's paragraph precedes the breezy journalist's commentary, which may be followed by the student's own highly colloquial addition. Similarly, you may come upon some suspiciously elevated vocabulary usages. "Thesaurusitis" is one source of this, to be sure, but a common source of such vocabulary is another writer, who should have been quoted rather than simply copied. Bjaaland and Lederman (1973, p. 203) note that scholarly adjectives in a freshman paper are common examples. They cite "torpid son," "degenerative aspects," and "meretricious doctrines." Other examples might be "tendentious remarks" or "cabalistic legislation." A query such as, "What do you mean by 'ineffable'?" can sometimes provide you with inexpressible information. Last, if you find that the paper uses several archaic terms, or words no longer used in the way the paper uses them, you may be looking at some very old text.

4.2.3 Long sentences.

What may at first appear to be a strange feature to be used as a clue to plagiarism can actually be very handy. Software analysis of student essays shows that college freshmen usually have an average sentence length of about 15 to 17 words. Women students are often a bit more verbally fluent than men, but the numbers are generally in that arena. With some practice, such as a good freshman composition class, sentence length can stretch out to 20 to 22 words or so on average. Compare this to an average length for Jonathan Swift in *Gulliver's Travels* of 38 words. As writers improve with practice, sentence structures tend to grow more complex and hence sentence lengths increase. (Note that there are exceptions, such as business prose and journalese, which set short sentences as a goal.) Generally, however, if the sentences of an entire paper or a section of a paper are unusually long, you may want to give the paper a second look for other clues to copying. Finally, if the sentences vary in average length by paragraph, that is also cause for concern. If some paragraphs feature sentences of an average of 15 words, while other paragraphs have 28-word sentences on average, there's your clue.

"Looks like someone turned in another copy of 'Deconstructing Michelangelo'. Mayfield has _never_ liked that paper."

✓ 4.3 KNOW THE MAJOR SOURCES OF PAPERS.

Before you begin to search for the source or sources of a suspect paper, you should know where to look. The following are the major sources of text in electronic form.

4.3.1 Local sources.

A roommate's or friend's disk is a common source of recycled papers. Organized student housing groups may also be keeping databases of papers for members' use.

Anecdote 4.3.1.1

I would like my professors to stay aware of plagiarized papers, because it is so easy to plagiarize a paper. The information is sitting right in front of us—on the Internet, in books, previous students' papers or essays. We have access to all of this information more easily than the professors can only imagine.

– Charity Cedarholm, university freshman

4.3.2 Free and for-sale term paper sites.

There are actually hundreds of these sites now, with some featuring thousands of papers each. See Appendix E for an annotated list of many of these sites, both those that offer free papers and those that sell papers. To see how easy it is to get a paper, and to canvass the quality and style you will find, you may want to visit a few of these sites.

4.3.3 The free, visible Web.

This category includes all the publicly mounted Web pages, which are indexed by search engines. Also called the surface Web, there are a few billion pages mounted now, and the best search engines each cover perhaps a third of it. To search as much as possible, you must use several search engines. Directories are also useful means of getting to information on this part of the Web. See Appendix D, Sections D.1, D.2, and D.3, for lists of search engines and directories.

4.3.4 Newsgroups.

Newsgroups contain threaded discussions and commentary on thousands of topics. The text of newsgroups is accessible either directly in the groups or by some search engines and by newsgroup engines such as Deja.com. Opinion appears to be growing that newsgroups are deteriorating into "spam warehouses"—repositories of junk mail—but a search there may prove profitable.

4.3.5 The free, deep Web.

Also called the invisible Web, this category includes the contents of sites that provide articles free to users, but the content may be accessible only by going directly to the site. That is, the articles are not indexed by search engines and therefore cannot be located by using a search engine. Some magazines, newspapers, reference works, encyclopedias, and subject-specific sites are in this category. According to BrightPlanet, the invisible or deep Web is about 500 times as large as the visible Web, which means hundreds of billions of pages (Bergman, 2000). Appendix D, Section D.4 provides a list of specific directories for help in accessing deep Web content.

4.3.6 Paid databases over the Web.

This category includes commercial databases for consumers (such as Electric Library and Northern Light's Special Collection) and databases that libraries subscribe to, containing scholarly journals, newspapers, court cases, and the like. Providers like Lexis-Nexis, UMI ProQuest, InfoTrac, JSTOR, and others are in this group. To find information from this category, you must have access to the database (through password or an on-campus computer) and search on the database directly.

4.3.7 CD-ROM resources.

Encyclopedias and some databases are available on CD-ROM. Many encyclopedias, especially Encarta, Grolier, and Compton's, have been given away free with computer purchases. Because the text is electronic, it can be copied just as easily as text on the Web. It might serve you well to own several of the more common of these encyclopedias.

✓ 4.4 CHECK LOCALLY.

Even with the advent of the Internet and easily downloadable papers and articles, a significant source of plagiarized papers is the friend or acquaintance on campus. See Anecdote 4.3.1.1 in this chapter and under Cartoon 10 in Appendix G. Students may be asking for the paper for your class.

4.4.1 Check your personal files.

If you have been keeping a copy of each paper submitted to you, you should have a file of papers to check against "new" submissions. Keeping them in electronic form so that they can be indexed and searched quickly is ideal, but even a filing cabinet divided by subject should be quickly accessible.

4.4.2 Check departmental or institutional databases.

If your department or institution keeps a file or database of submitted papers, and if your students know about it, there will be less likelihood of their passing the papers on down. An electronic database and electronic submitted paper can be compared by the Wordcheck software application. See Section 4.6.5 below.

✓ 4.5 SEARCH FOR THE PAPER ON-LINE.

If you suspect the paper may have come from the Web or an on-line database, you might want to search for it personally. Alternatively, ask your department to appoint a graduate student to a research assistant position, to be trained as a plagiarism detective. Another good long-term strategy is to lobby for an extra research librarian who can become an expert in hunting down suspected plagiarism. In either case, a person with such training and experience would be a valuable resource and would be able to locate sources rapidly. One inhibitor to running down suspected plagiarism is the time and effort involved. Many more faculty would no doubt be willing to chase cheaters if such a resource person were available. Meanwhile, remember that many current librarians are both willing and able to assist you in searching for and verifying the sources of suspect papers. For searching on your own, some strategies are listed below.

4.5.1 Try Findsame.

First, go to Findsame (http://www.findsame.com) a powerful content-search engine, and type or paste in a suspect paragraph or document up to 50 kilobytes in size. Findsame will return a list of matching pages, ranked by percent of sameness. You can even view your suspect text and the matching texts side by side for comparison.

4.5.2 Try HowOriginal.

HowOriginal.com (http://www.howoriginal.com) is a free service of Integriguard. Users may copy and paste or type in up to one kilobyte of text and HowOriginal will compare it with text on the Web. Users then receive an e-mail with the URL of a report listing matches on a sentence-by-sentence basis, together with the URLs of the locations of the matches. The company plans to add an internal database of mill papers soon.

4.5.3 Try EssayCrawler.

EssayCrawler (http://www.essaycrawler.com) is a metasearch tool for free term papers, with a database of tens of thousands of papers from several paper mill sites. By typing in three or four keywords, the subject, or the title from a suspect paper, you can search the offerings of all these sites at once.

4.5.4 Try EssayFinder.

EssayFinder (http://www.essayfinder.com) is a search tool for tens of thousands of commercially available papers ($9.85 per page as of this writing). Searching of a few keywords will bring up a list of available titles, together with a 50- to 75-word annotation describing the contents, including length. The information given in the description may be enough for you to match the paper with your questioned document.

4.5.5 Use a metasearch tool.

Metasearch tools allow you to search for a text string using several search engines at one time. With a search engine, you can look for a four- to six-word exact phrase unusual enough to fingerprint the paper. Searching for an exact title is a type of text search that sometimes pinpoints the paper quickly.

You can also look for a subject, together with the words "essay," "research paper," or "term paper," as in "treatment of schizophrenia research paper." For searches like this, it is better not to use an exact phrase search, but simply type in all these words in the search box. This method often locates papers at paper mill sites offering free papers.

Popular metasearch tools include Dogpile and Mamma. See Appendix D, Section D.2, for URLs and a discussion.

4.5.6 Use several search engines.

If you find nothing with the tools above, try a "six-shooter" of large-database, full-text search engines: Google, Northern Light, Fast, AltaVista, HotBot, and Lycos would be one sample set. At each, perform a search on a four- to six-word phrase from a suspect part of the paper (find a phrase that has two or three relatively unusual words in it) or a subject search as described just above. Remember that no search engine covers more than about a third of the visible Web (even the engines indexing more than a billion pages), so you should try several engines before you give up. You may discover through experience that particular engines are especially effective for finding copied papers in the subject areas you assign.

As already mentioned, Appendix D contains an annotated list of search engines, directories, and other tools for helping you look for suspect text on the Web.

Example 4.5.6.1

A free paper from each of three mill sites was downloaded: one on *Gulliver's Travels* from Cheater.com, one on *Great Expectations* from Schoolsucks.com, and one on *The Red Badge of Courage* from Totally.net. The search strings used were "poking fun at talking horses," "character who was called Compeyson," and "battle a fearful youth" except for EssayCrawler, where the papers were searched for by book titles. As can be seen in the table below, this rather unscientific sample search reveals that the particular essay on *Gulliver's Travels* has been republished on several paper sites (the sites encouraging plagiarism are plagiarizing each other!) and that EssayCrawler was the single successful source for finding all three papers. As we are always being reminded, "Your mileage may vary," depending on the subject and the paper. It is also important to note that you may locate *a* source for a plagiarized paper without locating *the* source used by the student. The fact that the paper is not original is the pertinent issue; the exact source is less critical.

Table of results for Example 4.5.6.1

Search Type	Results		
	Gulliver's Travels	*Great Expectations*	*Red Badge*
Findsame	6 matches	no match	no match
HowOriginal	3 matches	no match	no match
EssayCrawler	matched	matched	matched
Google	15 matches	no match	no match
Northern Light	4 matches	no match	no match
Fast Search	4 matches	no match	no match
AltaVista	4 matches	no match	no match
HotBot	3 matches	no match	no match
Lycos	4 matches	no match	no match
MetaCrawler	2 matches	no match	1 match
Dogpile	13 matches	no match	1 match
Mamma	2 matches	no match	1 match

4.5.7 Check on-line journals.

In addition to the journals in proprietary databases (discussed below), many journals are available over the Web free and without any restricted access. To check these journals, use a directory, such as Yahoo, Looksmart, or Snap and search for "on-line journals" or a more specific category, such as "ethics journals," depending on your subject area. Journal articles are fertile ground for wholesale copying because they are scholarly, well researched, and fully footnoted.

4.5.8 Check the deep Web.

Locate some appropriate databases on the deep Web (see Section 4.3.5), depending on the subject of the paper. Appendix D,

Section D.4 lists some of the sites that provide links to many of these databases. If indicated, visit some of the on-line encyclopedias as well. (See Appendix D, Section D.6, for sites linking to encyclopedias.) Here, you will have to use keyword searches rather than exact phrase searches, but using a string of appropriate keywords can be very powerful.

You might want to develop a list of sites specific to your discipline or to the topics you normally assign and set up links to those sites on a Web page so that you can visit each one quickly. For example, there are several "book notes" sites that students are likely to steal from in introductory literature classes because the sites provide analyses of novels and themes. (See Appendix D, Section D.10, for examples of these sites.) Some research using a good directory or two, or perhaps a search engine, will help you locate the sites pertinent to your area.

4.5.9 Check newsgroups.

Since some students may ask for help on newsgroups and then copy the replies, or since they may go to the newsgroups and copy whatever appears to fit, looking there may prove successful. Deja.com is currently the single best source for searching newsgroup content (http://www.deja.com). You can either go to a particular newsgroup or search on all of them.

4.5.10 Check proprietary databases.

Now try both Web commercial databases such as Northern Light's Special Collection and your library's on-line database subscriptions and search on subject-appropriate databases using keyword searches. InfoTrac, ProQuest, Lexis-Nexis, JSTOR, and many other commercial databases are examples of places to look. In spite of what may seem to be an endless number of journals, the subject of the paper will narrow down your search focus. Keyword searching will make the hunt even easier. Librarians are quite adept with on-line databases, so their assistance will be especially helpful here.

4.5.11 Check paper mill sites.

Appendix E lists dozens of paper mill sites, some offering free papers and others selling them. While it would be an arduous task to visit every site, some sites (such as those operated by The Paper Store) seem to have connected databases, while others (the free sites) appear to have many of the same papers. Checking a few of the larger sites might be worthwhile.

✓ 4.6 USE A PLAGIARISM DETECTOR.

If you do not find the paper as a result of searches conducted as described above, you might want to turn to commercial services that provide plagiarism detection. Several of the more prominent services are described here.

4.6.1 Plagiarism.org.

Plagiarism.org (http://www.plagiarism.org) provides an on-line service that checks uploaded student papers against a large database and provides reports of results. The company has added many of the free papers from term paper mills to its database, together with much Web content. To use the service, an instructor registers a class. Students in the class are then required to upload their papers to the site, where the software compares the papers to the database and produces an originality report. Articles linked to the site report that the service has met with considerable success, as well as much media publicity. At the time of writing, free trials were available, and a subscription for a course was fairly economical.

"You use a software program to check for plagiarized papers? Oh, man, that is *so* sneaky! Isn't that unethical or something?"

4.6.2 Integriguard.

Integriguard (http://www.integriguard.com) offers Paperbin.com (http://www.paperbin.com), a service similar to that of

Plagiarism.org in that after an instructor or institution registers a course, students upload their papers to the site, which checks them and sends an e-mail report to the instructor. Papers are compared against an internal database of papers as well as Web content. Again, pricing is fairly economical.

4.6.3 Eve2.

Eve2 (http://www.canexus.com/eve/index.shtml) is an inexpensive software agent designed especially for plagiarism detection, which installs on a local computer. Papers are entered either in plain text or in Word or WordPerfect format. The program then searches the Web to compare the paper with Internet content. The search result shows the site(s) and the degree of match. This program might be thought of as a special purpose metasearch tool.

4.6.4 Lexibot.

Lexibot (http://www.lexibot.com) is a moderately priced metasearch tool that uses more than five hundred search engines, from both the visible and the deep Web. If your department or institution employs a dedicated search professional, this will be an important tool in the battle against plagiarism. Since it is designed as a search tool, it is also valuable for research. The site has a list of the database search engines it currently uses.

4.6.5 Wordcheck.

Wordcheck (http://www.wordchecksystems.com) offers a software application installed at the local institution. The program performs keyword counting and displays comparative information. Thus, word patterns can be matched. An institution would create its own local database of papers or texts, together with their keyword profiles. This program appears to be more complex than some of the other solutions.

Notes:

Chapter 5

Strategies for Dealing with Plagiarism

My books need no title or judge to prove them; your page stares you in the face and says, "You are a thief!"

– Martial, Epigrams, I.53

If you have followed the advice in the early chapters of this book to provide clear education and careful assignments, you should have relatively few cases of plagiarism to deal with, and those you do have should be free of many of the complicating ambiguities and excuses that might otherwise occur. Nevertheless, there will be occasions when you need to meet with a suspected plagiarist to determine the truth. When you are ready to deal with a case of plagiarism, you have either overwhelming evidence, such as a mill paper that exactly matches the student's submission, or you have strong enough suspicions to bring the student in for a discussion of the matter. This chapter provides strategies for dealing with both situations.

✓ 5.1 PREPARE FOR THE INTERACTION.

The best way to make an interaction go as smoothly and effectively as possible is to be well prepared for it. Emotionally charged meetings need clear structure if they are to maintain orderliness and a sense of objectivity. The value of knowing the rules and having a plan cannot be overstated.

5.1.1 Review all policies, rules, and guidelines.

Before you meet with the student, review your institution's academic honesty policy (often found in the student handbook) and any policies about cheating or plagiarism from your department. Also, reread your own syllabus for the course to be sure that you have the wording clear in your mind. Exact knowledge of policies and processes will give you a greater flexibility as you work with the student, who may have several creative turns in store for you. A student may plead ignorance, claim the prohibition or definition of plagiarism is ambiguous, attempt to interpret policy to exonerate himself or herself, or try some other maneuver based on written rules.

5.1.2 Follow due process.

Many colleges and universities have specific steps that must be followed in cases of accusations of academic dishonesty: reporting procedures, list of persons who must be informed, the rights of the student to see evidence or interview witnesses in advance, the procedure for appeals, and so forth. As you review the policies mentioned in the section above, keep the idea of due process in mind and be sure to adhere to the appropriate steps. Remember also to follow institutional requirements for confidentiality.

5.1.3 Remember you may be wrong.

Depending on their personalities and style, some professors are intentionally rough on students accused of cheating, hoping to scare them out of committing the act again. Others try to make the meeting a redemptive one in an attempt to salvage the academic attitudes and performance of the student. Depending on the nature of the cheating and the history of the student, both these approaches or some other approach may be good. However, before taking any approach that assumes guilt, it is better to treat all accused students with respect and dignity, taking an "innocent-until-proven-guilty" stance. Such an approach is, of course, (1) just and fair, (2) legally smart, and (3) psychologically smart, to prevent damaging an innocent person with denunciations, but it is also (4) quite prudent (in Aristotle's practical sense) because you may just be wrong. Whatever the evidence looks like, wait until you hear the student's explanation. And it may be ultimately more effective to fail a student in your course (if that is the penalty under the situation) with a tone of sadness and regret than with a tone of vengefulness (even if the latter is how you feel for being so put upon).

Anecdote 5.1.3.1

Two upstanding students I know were falsely accused of plagiarism by a teacher with a reputation for getting kids into trouble. This accusation affected them personally. It affected their work for other classes, their reputations, and their relationships with other teachers as well as students.

– Kristina Petrosino, university freshman

5.1.4 Remember how varied plagiarism is.

Depending on the amount of evidence you have and what kind of training you have presented in class, you might not know how intentional the plagiarism was. A student who, through ignorance or confusion, clumsily copied a few sentences or a paragraph, is not the same kind of person as the student who engaged in "authorship by Visa" and simply bought a paper from a mill. It may be counterproductive to treat harshly a student who would not knowingly cheat. On the other hand, treating even the guiltiest with kindness at the outset allows you to gather more evidence and build your case before you show your hand.

5.1.5 Verify evidence from third parties.

If you use software reports from a service or an in-house software application, verify the copying by a personal look at the source and copied texts. If the source is on the Web, go to the site(s) and print off the document(s). If a student tells you that a paper was copied from his or her disk, try to obtain the disk or the file in question or, at the least, a printout of the file.

5.1.6 Be sure all evidence and records are safely locked up.

If you leave your office unlocked during the day, be sure you have a secure filing cabinet or other locked source for the evidence. Even if you keep your office locked, many campuses hire student maintenance and housekeeping workers (who have master keys), so that you should always have some unique-key secure area for evidence and old papers. Keep copies of electronic data on floppies, zip disks, or CD-RWs or even e-mail them to yourself so that they can reside safely somewhere outside of your office. Securely locked evidence protects against theft and against the violation of students' privacy. While a case is still in the investigative stage, no one else need know—especially by accident—what you suspect.

5.1.7 Have the evidence ready for the meeting.

Whether the student has engaged in inappropriate paraphrasing (that you think may have come from ignorance) or wholesale stealing of another paper, have the evidence with you, but not visible on the table. You might want to make your claim in general terms, such as, "I am concerned about the authorship of this paper," and then get the student's story before bringing out the evidence. After the student's explanation, show the evidence and then see what happens to the story. This process can go far to reveal how guilty or ignorant the student really is (though, of course, some students will bluff ignorance).

5.1.8 Consider the presence of a colleague.

Depending on the nature of the copying, the personality of the student, and the penalty you have in mind, you may want to have a witness present at the meeting. If your institution has a hearing process, then you are already set. A student facing expulsion from the university may take some desperate measures that might impact your own reputation. ("I told him I would do anything not to fail this course, and he said. . . .")

The presence of more than one other person might not be advisable because of the resulting distraction and because additional persons will intensify the pressure on the student, creating more anxiety than necessary and possibly increasing the student's hostility and lack of cooperation. There are also privacy considerations to be made with additional witnesses. Your department or divisional chair or school dean provides a logical additional person to be in on the discussion.

5.1.9 Recognize your legal standing.

Fear of the possibility of a lawsuit over an accusation of plagiarism can make faculty hesitant to go forward with appropriate charges. Following your institution's due process procedures carefully can reduce your exposure. If you believe that any part of the procedures is ambiguous, you should seek clarification from an appropriate administrator or from your college's legal counsel.

A recent article posted on the Web by an attorney who specializes in higher-education law includes a short discussion of how faculty have little or no liability for reporting plagiarism if it is done in good faith (Standler, 2000). However, keep in mind that laws vary among jurisdictions and their interpretations are constantly changing, so what may be solid legal advice at one point in time in one place may be poor at a later point or in another place.

✓ 5.2 BEGINNING THE INTERACTION.

What happens in the first minute or two of the meeting may make all the difference between an effective truth-finding session with the cooperation of the student and an angrily hostile reaction that precludes making a satisfactory determination. As you expect the student to be calm, be calm yourself.

5.2.1 Treat the student with respect.

In a court of law, even individuals accused of the most heinous crimes are treated with respect. Likewise, you should treat a student you suspect of engaging in plagiarism with respect, even if you abhor the suspected misconduct. Avoid raising your voice; avoid scolding or overly admonishing the student. Your goal is to help the student grow into a responsible adult. Despite his or her failure to abide by the rules in this particular matter, he or she may have many other wonderful qualities that may be developed through a college education. Despite this admonition, established penalties should be applied equally in all cases, without favoritism. Remember that the other side of favoritism is discrimination.

5.2.2 Read the rules to the student.

Some faculty find that sitting down in the office with a student and merely reading the section on cheating or plagiarism from the student handbook results in a sobbing confession—sometimes a confession of even more than the faculty member suspects. Faculty who follow this process should give the student a photocopy and then read from another copy as the student follows along. After reading, the instructor might say, "Now is there anything you want to tell me?" or perhaps, "Is there anything you want to say about your research paper?"

If you do not have strong evidence and only suspect the student of plagiarizing, it may be better to skip this action and go directly to the questions.

"Well, Merkins, I must admit I'm impressed by this paper. In fact, I wish I'd written it myself. No doubt you wish you had, too."

How *not* to begin a discussion about suspected plagiarism.

5.2.3 Ask questions rather than make accusations.

Recall the complexities of the situation. The student may have been ignorant of the proper citation rules (unless you have precluded this) or inadvertently copied (unless you have trained the class well). Even if you have two identical copies of a paper, the student in your office may be the victim of theft rather than the perpetrator of the fraud (that is, his or her original paper may have been stolen by another student). By asking questions, you are more likely to discover the real situation. Many students, when they get the drift of your questions, will (if guilty) break down and confess.

In situations where you only suspect and do not have strong evidence, questions will be much more effective than accusations. In fact, Lisa Renard (1999) argues that unanswerable evidence is not needed if the questions are posed carefully. If the student cannot demonstrate authorship by answering questions about the content, main points, research strategies, and sources, then the instructor has grounds enough to ask the student to rewrite the paper. On the other hand, if the student can provide acceptable answers, the matter can be dropped.

✓ 5.3 DISTINGUISHING TRUTH FROM DECEPTION.

> Most liars can fool most people most of the time.
> – Paul Ekman, *Telling Lies*

If determining when another person is lying to us were a simple and exact process, the world we live in would be a much different place. (We would at least need to accommodate ourselves to others' real opinions of our neckties or earrings.) The detection of deception is an inexact science—or an art—depending on experience as well as knowledge. Some people are much better deceivers than others and some instructors learn to become much better at detection than others. That said, a substantial amount of research has gone into the area of identifying behavioral cues that reveal deception. Several recent books, including those by Ekman (1992), Vrij (2000), Hausman (1999), Lieberman (1998), and Ford (1996) are available to explain the techniques for distinguishing truth from deception.

5.3.1 Be circumspect about the evidence you use.

The use of "water cooler opinion" about how to determine when a student is lying can be misleading and unreliable. Keep in mind the following:

(a) There is no single, certain sign of deception. You must use a set of indicators and draw a judgment from them (Shoemaker, 1997).

(b) Many commonly believed signs of deception are not at all reliable. These include eye movements, posture, look of sorrow, and so on (Porter, 2000).

(c) Many supposed signs of deception are actually signs of nervousness, fear, or anger. These include fidgeting, playing with objects (pen, paper clip, hair), dry mouth, drained face, high-pitched voice, and so on (Ekman, 1992). Nervousness can result from many causes, including simply being called into a professor's office. (Of course, nervousness can also be connected to an attempt at deception.)

(d) The better you know the student and his or her habits of speech and behavior under normal (or "baseline") conditions, the more accurate you can be in evaluating the cues displayed during an interview about plagiarism.

5.3.2 Remember that deception may occur in several forms.

A liar may feel guilty about lying or may fear being caught. As a result, he or she may use statements that are intended to mislead but are not literally false. For instance, Example 5.3.2.1 illustrates a statement that may be only a half-truth created by omitting some details and giving only part of the story.

Example 5.3.2.1

"Did you copy this paper?"
"A friend showed me his paper as a guideline."

Example 5.3.2.2 illustrates what might be a deflected answer.

Example 5.3.2.2

"Did you copy this paper?"
"I did my best to cite every source."

Example 5.3.2.3 illustrates how a student might attempt to change the topic.

Example 5.3.2.3

"Did you copy this paper?"
"This is about punctuation and mechanics, isn't it? I was never good at those."

✓ 5.4 QUESTIONING TECHNIQUES.

This section provides you with a number of choices for asking questions about the student's work and research process. Most of the questions involve an indirect approach rather than a confrontational approach. We are thus, in effect, taking the advice of Polonius:

> And thus do we of wisdom and of reach,
> With windlasses and with assays of bias,
> By indirections find directions out.
> – Hamlet, II.i

5.4.1 Provide an environment for telling the truth.

By creating the right psychological environment, you can increase the probability of getting a confession from the guilty. Here are three suggestions: First, raise the stakes for lying. By letting the student know that lying to you is an offense in itself, in addition to the plagiarizing, you give the guilty another reason to be honest with you. Second, consider using neutral words or euphemisms. Few students will want to confess to "cheating," "lying," "stealing," or "plagiarizing," at least not at first. The guilty will be more likely to admit to "copying," "not citing," or "using someone else's paper." The following two examples illustrate this suggestion:

Example 5.4.1.1

"Did you copy some of this paper from somewhere?"
"Well, yes."
"Did you copy most of it from other places?"
"Uh huh."

Example 5.4.1.2

"Don't these words need to have quotation marks around them?"
"I guess so."
"Because these words came from another source, and you didn't write them?"
"Yeah."

The third suggestion is to ask questions that will relax the innocent but worry the guilty. The following example illustrates this:

Example 5.4.1.3

"I'm sorry if this process makes you nervous. If you help me figure this out, we can be finished quickly. Will you help me with that?"

Allow the student to talk freely once you ask for an explanation. Do not interrupt or contradict, but let the full story come out. The more details you get, the more evidence of guilt, deception, or innocence you will obtain. You can return to various parts of the story later on in order to rebut them.

5.4.2 Ask nonspecific questions.

It is sometimes said that the best plagiarism detector is the student who handed in the paper because he or she already knows whether the paper is genuine or what part is fraudulent. Because few students are hardened cheaters, many will break down at the first suspicion that they have been caught. Therefore, you can sometimes ask a question that seems to imply that the student has been caught, to see what happens. Such a question is useful because you must be very careful about accusing a student of cheating unless you have very strong evidence. A false accusation can be both cruel and reason for litigation. A question of high implication, though, is relatively safe. Here are some sample questions that may help reveal the truth, and that can be asked even before you read the cheating rules to the student:

➢ "Tell me about this paper."

➢ "Do you have something to tell me about this paper?"

➢ "I was surprised by your paper, so I did some investigation into it. Before I tell you what I found out, is there anything you want to tell me about it?"

➢ "I'm curious to know why your writing style is so good in some parts of the paper and so poor in others. And why have you not shown such great writing on the in-class essays?"

➢ "This long passage doesn't sound like your normal style. Is this a quotation where you accidentally forgot the quotation marks?"

5.4.3 Ask questions about plagiarizing.

The almost repetitious nature of these questions gives the student the opportunity to change his or her mind at some point and confess, and their variations may produce a different confession from what your suspicions have led you to expect. Here are some examples:

➢ "Did you write this paper?"

➢ "Did you write all of it?"

➢ "Did someone help you write or edit this? The Writing Center? A tutor? Give me an example of how the tutor helped you."

➢ "Did you cite every reference you used?"

➢ "Are you familiar with the rules of paraphrasing? You understand that you must still cite a source even though you put the author's ideas into your own words?" (Here you may begin to distinguish between ignorance and intentionality.)

➢ "So you're saying that you did not knowingly copy any entire sentences or paragraphs without citing them?" (Note how this question may seem to imply that you have some evidence to the contrary.)

➢ "I know some people think that it's too much trouble or too picky to use quotation marks for just a couple of words. What about you? Did you include any short phrases that you didn't quote and cite?"

➢ "This whole paragraph sounds like a quotation to me. Did you forget to use a block indentation on it or did you write it yourself?"

➢ "When did you write this paper?" (This is a good question if you suspect the paper may be a recycle from earlier terms or years.)

5.4.4 Ask questions about content.

The student who turns in a wholesale copying job (a download or a friend's paper) may not even have read it, so you might begin simply by asking for clarification of meaning. Questions about central themes, the flow of the argument, and particular words can be helpful in getting at the truth. Here are some example types of questions about content:

➢ "What exactly do you mean here by 'dynamic equivalence'?"

➢ "In what sense are you using 'soporific' here?"

➤ "I can't quite separate the argument here. Are you making two points or only one here? Explain."

A useful type of content question is the reversal question. Ask the student to explain a particular argument in the paper, but phrase the question in a way that implies the opposite of what has actually been expressed in the paper. For example, if in a paper on energy conservation the student argues that the cost of solar heating is reasonable, ask why he or she argues that it is not reasonable. The honest student, who knows the paper and its argument, will correct your "misinterpretation."

"Parts of this paper are really very good, but I must say that the final third is rather unclear to me."

"Yeah, I didn't understand that part either...it, er...heh...I...er... mean... *gulp!*"

5.4.5 Ask questions about sources.

Whether you suspect a wholesale copy, stolen citations, or fabricated citations, asking about the sources can be useful. You might ask the student to review the research methods used, to identify the sources, or where they were found. If you have followed the advice in Chapter 3, you will already have required that copies of sources be submitted with the paper, thus easing the process of asking questions about them. In such a case, your questions will determine only how familiar the student is with the sources, not whether they have been faked. Example questions:

➤ "Tell me how you researched and wrote this paper. What process did you use?"

➤ "Where did you look for your sources? Which libraries or databases did you consult?"

➤ "Did you find this book in our library?"

➤ "Where did you find the article by Edwards? It sounds fascinating. Can you bring me a copy at the next meeting?"

➤ "This quotation seems slightly out of context. What was Follet's main point in the chapter?"

➤ "I see you made extensive use of Tom Freland's book on welfare. What is your overall opinion of the book? Where did you locate a copy? What did you think of his argument that welfare is a political rather than an economic problem?"

Be aware that some students may say (either quite honestly or otherwise) that they went home over a break (Thanksgiving, three-day weekend, Christmas, etc.) and used resources in a local public or college library. If you choose to check out this claim, you can get the name of the library and the city and either search that library's on-line catalog or call to see if such a book or journal is held there. You may even be able to ask a librarian there to verify the pages for you. (If you ask the student, "Did you check out the book or use it in the library?" a guilty student will probably just prevaricate and claim to have used it in the library.) To check the source itself, you can get the same book through interlibrary loan if your institution does not own it. (Again, the better remedy is to ask for copies of all sources with the final draft of the paper. See Chapter 3, Section 3.2.6.)

✓ 5.5 BE PREPARED FOR RATIONALIZATIONS.

Whether through confession or the demonstration of extremely strong evidence, students who eventually admit to plagiarizing will often present some reason (or excuse, defense, justification, or explanation), all the while claiming, "I never intended to plagiarize." In this section, you will find a list of many of the standard excuses students might give. A good way to prevent having to deal with most of the following is to have a class discussion about them and explain early in the course of instruction why they are not acceptable. Below are examples of reasons students might give and responses you might consider using:

5.5.1 The plagiarism was someone else's fault.

Examples of *reasons* students give that put the blame on someone else include these:

➤ My typist left out the quotation marks.

➤ My typist forgot to block indent that quotation.

➤ My typist left out the citation.

➤ I was taught to do it that way in high school.

➤ The tutor in the Writing Center told me it was okay.

➤ I showed this to another professor, and she said this was correct.

➤ The computer crashed when I was writing the paper and must have lost the citation.

➤ I put the citations in last but must have accidentally saved an older version over a newer version when I backed up the disk and then turned in the wrong version. [Note that this reason implies that the correct version cannot be turned in because it was erased in the accident.]

The following is an example of a *response* an instructor might give when a student blames someone else:

➤ You, not your typist, peer editor, the Writing Center, or the professor—you and you alone—are ultimately responsible for your paper. That includes grammar and mechanics and accurate quotation and citation. It is impossible to know what the paper looked like when it was shown to someone else, under what circumstance the other person looked at it (one minute in the hallway?), or what was said. All we have is the paper you submitted, which seems to reveal plagiarism.

5.5.2 The plagiarism was the professor's fault.

Examples of *reasons* that students give to blame the professor include these:

➤ You said we could work together, so we wrote a joint paper.

➤ You are the only professor that does not allow this.

➤ I had you look at my paper and you said it looked okay.

➤ I showed it to you after class one day and you didn't say anything then.

➤ I listed the book in the bibliography, so you could have looked it up.

➤ You didn't teach me that stuff in a way I could understand.

The following is an example of a *response* an instructor might give when a student blames someone else:

➢ Point to the statement in your syllabus regarding all students doing their own, individual work, and noting that collaboration is limited to proofing help, idea generation, and so on. Again relevant is the statement that the student bears ultimate responsibility for the paper. Plagiarism may not be discerned by a brief glance. (It may be wise to caution students that if you agree to look at the paper in advance, they are not automatically thereafter absolved of responsibility for errors, omissions, or plagiarism later discovered therein.)

5.5.3 The plagiarism resulted from ignorance or confusion.

Examples of *reasons* students give that put the blame on ignorance or confusion include these:

➢ I didn't know you had to use quotes if you cited the source.

➢ I thought the information was common knowledge and didn't require citation.

➢ I confused my notes and forgot which words were my own thoughts and which were quotations.

➢ I thought that was an acceptable way to paraphrase.

The following is an example of a *response* an instructor might give when a student blames someone else:

➢ Point to the explanations and training you have given in class about what needs to be cited. A handout or Web page with several examples is ideal, so that there can be no confusion about exactly what was demonstrated.

5.5.4 The plagiarism resulted from insidious causes.

Here is an example of a *reason* students give that puts the blame on insidious causes:

➤ I put in the citation, so you can see I didn't cheat intentionally.

Note that this must be a clever technique taught in some book on how to cheat. The student plagiarizes, copies a paragraph, perhaps two, word for word but includes the citation at the end of the plagiarized material. If the paper passes by and the instructor does not catch it, the student gets away with the offense. If the instructor checks and finds the plagiarism, the student has a built-in excuse and "proof" of innocence, or at least purity of intention. To be fair, under some circumstances, this could be an honest claim from an ignorant or mistaught student. Educational sessions at the beginning of the semester should preclude both the cunning act and the ignorant one.

The following is another example of a *reason* that students give that puts the blame on insidious causes:

➤ But if I cited everything I used, my paper would be nothing but citations.

Note that this explanation implies that a paper should be little more than an esthetic object, one that looks good with a nice balance of citations and plain text, regardless of what has been borrowed or even quoted. The response might be to explain that first, every borrowing must be cited regardless of the perceived appearance it produces, and that if indeed this would result in "nothing but citations," the student is evidently not doing sufficient thinking or adding adequate analysis to the paper. Sources should support the student's words, not vice versa. (How unfortunate it is that many students use their words merely as transitional glue to hold their sources together.)

5.5.5 Miscellaneous reasons.

Examples of other *reasons* that students give for submitting a plagiarized paper include these:

➢ We wrote it together to save time.

➢ The book said it better than I could, so I used those words.

➢ In my native country, this is acceptable.

➢ Everybody else in class (school, country, world) is doing the same thing.

In response, you might point to the rules of the course. Those rules apply regardless of the student's time-saving values, a preference for another's words over one's own, the rules of another country or culture, or the perceived cheating habits of others.

"Dear Mr. Trent: Since you only *pretended* to write this paper, I only *pretended* to grade it!"

It is probably best to write only, "See me," on papers you suspect have been plagiarized.

✓ 5.6 TEST THE STUDENT.

If the student continues to deny plagiarizing but you still have strong suspicions after your conversation, you can test the student more formally. Bringing up the idea of a test and administering the test itself should occur in the same session so the student will not have the opportunity to read the paper carefully and memorize its contents. The test, therefore, should be prepared in advance if possible.

5.6.1 Give a content test.

A content test can be structured like an ordinary test, using multiple-choice questions, fill-in-the-blank, short essay, or even true-false questions. By covering the major points, names of people, organizations, objects, ideas, events, or situations, you will be able to determine how familiar the student is with the paper. If the questions go beyond the paper but cover what the student would most likely have encountered in researching the material, you will gain an even better idea about authorship. An innocent student will probably not get a perfect score, but should know most of the answers.

5.6.2 Give a modified cloze test.

A modified cloze test is created by taking the student's paper and deleting carefully selected key terms (that even a student with high reading comprehension could not supply without knowledge of the essay's content) and replacing the terms with fixed-length blank lines. The student is then asked to fill in all the blanks with the appropriate words. The accuracy of the fill-ins (using the original words, using synonyms of the original words, or using completely different words) and the time needed to complete the task will reveal the degree of familiarity with the text.

Example 5.6.2.1

Original text, with key terms underlined:

Information in possession of one side but not the other created an <u>information asymmetry</u>, resulting in a <u>power</u> advantage for those possessing the information. Because information is <u>power</u>, those who have information have <u>power</u>.

Modified cloze test for the student to fill in:

Information in possession of one side but not the other created an
_____ _____, resulting in a _____ advantage for those possessing the information. Because information is _____, those who have information have _____.

If the student wrote the words in the original text in Example 5.6.2.1, there should be enough clues in the cloze test to remind the student of the concept and the repetition of the word "power." On the other hand, if the student is not familiar with the paper, there would be no obvious reason to fill in the same word in the last three blanks.

5.6.3 Give a commercial cloze test.

The Glatt Plagiarism Screening Program from Glatt Software at Plagiarism.com (http://www.plagiarism.com) produces a cloze procedure automatically. The software converts a suspect essay into a fill-in text by deleting words and substituting blanks. The purported author of the essay then sits down at the computer and attempts to fill in the blanks with the original words. By calculating the accuracy of the fill-ins and the time taken to complete the procedure, the software then offers a probability-of-authorship rating. The company says that no student has been falsely accused based on these results. This CD-ROM software is available for local installation and use by the instructor.

✓ 5.7 CONSIDER THE PENALTY.

> So when the wicked receive punishment they receive something good, the punishment itself, which is good, because of its justice; but when they go unpunished they acquire some extra evil in actually going scot free, which you have agreed is bad, because of the injustice. . . . So the wicked are much more unhappy when they are unjustly allowed to go scot free, than when a just punishment is imposed upon them.
>
> – Boethius, *Consolation of Philosophy* IV,
> tr. V. E. Watts

Once you are convinced, either through confession or evidence, that the student has cheated, you must assess what penalty to give. The penalty depends on several factors.

5.7.1 Consider the nature of the offense.

Plagiarism encompasses a wide variety of improper behaviors, from careless citation practices and ignorant uses, to cynical copying of entire essays. For that reason, think first about the seriousness of the offense:

➢ Was this the first act of cheating?

➢ Are the reasons given by the student credible?

➢ How extensive is the plagiarism?

➢ What kind of plagiarism is it—verbatim, improper paraphrase, use of a unique idea?

5.7.2 Do not name the penalty immediately.

You may want to reflect on what the student has told you (and perhaps check out some of the story) or confer with colleagues (while remembering to protect the student's right to privacy) or the administration before you hand down a penalty. You may find it best, then, to tell the student you will think about the case and determine a penalty within a reasonable time (say three days to a week). You may also discover that the student will get in touch with you again before the time has elapsed and offer a revised story (perhaps confession or perhaps evidence of innocence).

5.7.3 Follow departmental policy.

As mentioned earlier, you should know and follow your institution's policies and how much leeway you have in assessing penalties. You should be aware of what standards should be applied in reaching the judgment that plagiarism has occurred when the student continues to deny it.

5.7.4 Consider the range of options between punishment and rehabilitation.

Is the offense of such a nature that making the student rewrite the paper for a lower grade would be ultimately better than failing the student in the course? Chapter 6 discusses a number of penalties, both punitive and rehabilitative, many of which would fall under the instructor's authority. See Section 6.4.

> According to a notion in Chinese popular religion there is a special section of hell in which teachers who have wronged their pupils by undue leniency must undergo punishment until this heavy sin is expiated!
>
> – Laurence G. Thompson, quoted in
> Bjaaland & Lederman (1973, p. 206).

Chapter 6

Administrative and Institutional Issues Relating to Plagiarism

There is much difference between imitating a man and counterfeiting him.

– Benjamin Franklin

The purpose of this chapter is to raise a number of issues relating to plagiarism and the institutional concerns surrounding it (and academic dishonesty in general), so that faculty and administrators can work together to develop effective and comprehensive policies and procedures. A set of uniform guidelines and equitable sanctions will make interactions between faculty and students over this issue easier for both. Students have a right to know the rules by which they will be judged: Being punished on the basis of an unannounced or unclear rule is not fair to them. Instructors need to know the process and sequence for handling academic dishonesty, including the scope and limits of their prerogatives, their range of options for penalties, and the steps of any allowed appeals. It is important for them to know to what extent the administration (departmental and institutional) supports their efforts to inhibit this kind of cheating. Investigating suspected plagiarism and confronting students about it is both laborious and stressful; if the administration will not support these efforts (as when clearly guilty students are let off), faculty need to know.

This chapter is not intended to provide a one-size-fits-all set of policies; rather, it is intended to raise questions and discuss possibilities and alternatives so that institutions can establish their own regulations.

✓ 6.1 CONSTRUCT CLEAR DEFINITIONS OF PLAGIARISM.

A common response of students confronted with evidence of plagiarism is the claim, "I didn't know that was plagiarism." In many cases, they may be telling the truth. The institution should therefore construct a set of clear definitions and examples so that "the law is clear." Here are some areas to consider:

6.1.1 Are the various kinds of plagiarism clearly explained?

Chapter 1, Section 1.2 covered many varieties of plagiarism, and these could be reviewed with students. Most students already know that some actions are clearly plagiarism:

➢ copying a paper from the Web

➢ copying a paper from a database

➢ submitting a friend's paper

However, other kinds of copying are less clearly wrong to them and should be spelled out in formal language:

➢ copying a writer verbatim without quotation marks

➢ inadequate paraphrasing, such as merely substituting synonyms while keeping syntax and other aspects the same

➢ rearranging another writer's words or sentences

➢ using another's ideas or facts without attribution

➢ using unique or apt phrases from another writer

➤ copying the organizational or syntactical structure of another writer

Your institution may want to distinguish several degrees of plagiarism. For example, first-degree plagiarism might include instances of obviously deliberate large-scale copying, as in the purchase or download of entire papers. Second-degree plagiarism might include carelessness in attribution or inadvertent plagiarism. Too many degrees would result in hairsplitting arguments, so caution should be exercised in making such distinctions. See also the discussion about "patchwriting" in Section 6.5.1 below.

6.1.2 Is self-recycling permitted or prohibited?

Self-recycling occurs when a student uses material from one paper in another paper. There are several forms of this:

➤ turning in the same paper to two (or more) different classes in the same term (often by writing a paper that meets both classes' topic requirements)

➤ turning in a paper written in a previous term

➤ using excerpts of previously written work to build on or incorporate into new work

Which, if any, of these activities should not be permitted? If a student uses an excerpt from a previous paper, should that be cited? Some institutions prohibit self-recycling under the reasoning that the purpose of assignments is not simply to complete them but to learn from them; thus, every assignment should involve new, original thinking and writing. On the other hand, many students believe that self-recycling is not wrong (see Appendix B, Section B.1, for further details). This is indeed an issue where institutional policy needs to be clear and widely publicized.

Anecdote 6.1.2.1

I don't believe you can plagiarize yourself. If you already have a printed idea and you express it again you're not stealing from anyone.

– Zachary Stred, university freshman

6.1.3 Is it permissible for a student to lend a paper to another as an example?

Using example papers is often done in classroom settings. What about among roommates or friends? Here are some issues:

➢ If a student lends a paper, who is responsible if the borrower plagiarizes it?

➢ Should lending of a printed copy be treated differently from lending a copy on disk or via e-mail?

➢ When a student shows a paper to another student to provide the student with an example, is that a praiseworthy instance of help-fulness and collaboration or is it abetting plagiarism?

Some institutions explicitly prohibit students from allowing others to copy work; however, in the case of a prosecution for plagiarism, how can the issue of willingness be firmly established? The original owner of the paper will most likely deny consenting to the copying. The issue of a printed versus an electronic original is barely worth distinguishing in an era of ubiquitous scanners and OCR software.

6.1.4 What constitutes the fair use of a tutor, writing assistant, or typist?

Most institutions have help systems to provide both weak and strong students with various services related to writing. Tutorial Centers, Writing Centers, Learning Resource Centers, all offer assistance. Students themselves are often eager to avail themselves of these services, and will allow the tutor to provide as much revising or even writing work as the tutor wants. Most instructors have probably had this experience themselves: Students often ask, "How should I say this?" or "How would you say it?" or "Which is the best word to use?" or "Can you outline this for me?" The gate-keeper for limiting the amount of help a student gets, then, is the helper. Absent a set of guidelines, some tutors may do too much work for a student, essentially engaging in ghostwriting. It is there-fore important at the institutional level to consider the limits of help permissible and to draw up a set of printed guidelines. Here are a few applicable questions to consider:

➢ How much grammar, editing, and writing assistance is permissi-ble?

➢ Can the tutor change sentence structure, correct spelling, or pro-vide research material?

➢ What are the limits of help with organization, outlining, choos-ing words or phrases?

➢ How is the help given by tutors to be monitored?

➢ Is there a set of printed guidelines for Writing Center and tutor-ing personnel?

6.1.5 Verify evidence from third parties.

Collaborative learning has risen to the ascendancy in many in-stitutions because students can learn well through the process. At the same time, academic integrity statements have sometimes not kept current with the complexities created by the use of this method. Some instructors permit or even require students to do re-search together, share resources they have located, engage in peer editing or quality circles, review each other's drafts and make sug-gestions, and so forth. However, unless there is a set of guidelines, students will not know the limits of this help and may end up in the instructor's office testily announcing they were told they could work together, which is why they wrote a joint paper. While some instructors may choose to formulate their own rules, where collaboration will vary depending on the nature of the class or even the assignment, some institutional help would be very useful. Here are a few relevant issues:

➤ If a peer editor makes a suggestion or offers an idea for further development, should the writer cite the peer as a source?

➤ May students working together share research sources (either URLs, bibliographic information, or printouts or copies of articles)? May they share books they have found?

The questions in Section 6.1.4 are equally relevant here for peer editors and collaborators.

Increasingly common at many institutions are joint projects, where a team writes a paper, works on a case study, or presents a report. These kinds of projects create complications for traditional definitions of plagiarism and the limits of collaboration. The policies established should take joint products into account. One way might be to require that all contributors to the project be listed as joint authors (whether researchers, writers, or editors, for example).

6.1.6 Who is responsible for cheating on a joint project?

An additional complication with joint projects may arise when one of the team members plagiarizes without the others' knowledge. If the professor discovers the plagiarism, what is the remedy? Many team efforts do not distinguish among who wrote what sections, and in some projects, one or more members of the team may work through the entire project, editing, adding, and deleting. Asking team members to keep track of who wrote what may be a useful idea.

"Hi, Jane. Sorry to bother you, but I'm just now making a paper and I'm all out of words. Could I borrow about 1200?"

✓ 6.2 PROCESSES.

Pursuing a case of plagiarism provides enough challenges without the added difficulty posed by unclear or undefined procedures. Students and faculty alike should have a definite process to follow.

6.2.1 Is there a set of clear procedures to be followed?

A clear, standard, university-wide set of policies and procedures is the ideal, where students taking courses from any discipline can know the rules. Due process has been mentioned in earlier discussions, and it bears mentioning here again. Remember that students have rights, including the following:

➢ the right to privacy

➢ the right to be considered innocent until proven guilty

➢ the right to a fair hearing

➢ the right to present a defense

➢ the right to appeal

Included in the rights above may be other rights, such as the right to examine evidence or interview witnesses. All faculty should be aware of these rights so that no student is treated unfairly.

Professors and students alike should be clear about the process of appeals and where the final determination of a contested accusation will be made.

6.2.2 Is plagiarism an academic or a disciplinary issue?

In a brief for the U.S. Department of Education, Sheilah Maramark and Mindi Barth Maline (1993) note that agreement over the very nature of the offense is lacking: "Confusion also exists among administrators as to whether cheating should be treated as part of disciplinary misconduct procedures or in the context of academic evaluation." Is plagiarizing part of the evaluation of student work in a course, and thus entirely an issue of instructor prerogative and management; or is it an institutional issue that needs to be processed by a disciplinary board or committee? This difference is important. An instructor may have more options for various punishments if the matter rests entirely within the course, while a student may have more guarantees of fairness if there is a hearing. On the other hand, even with ordinary grades, a student who feels that a grade is unjust has appeal mechanisms at most institutions.

If plagiarism is an academic issue:

➢ Can a professor's decision and grade be overridden? If so, by whom?

➢ What is the appeal process?

➢ Will the institution supply legal counsel if the professor is sued?

If plagiarism is a disciplinary issue:

➢ How is the cheating reported?

➢ Who evaluates the evidence?

➢ Are instructors permitted to circumvent the process if they believe a more equitable solution can be achieved privately?

➢ What are the channels of the decision and appeals?

6.2.3 How do departmental and institutional policies meld?

Uniform institutional policies may be the ideal, but departments may have varying attitudes toward plagiarism, varying definitions of what they consider unacceptable, and varying methods for punishing or remedying the problem. For institutions at the incipient stages of policy making in this area, a dialog among administrators and departments is crucial.

6.2.4 How much instructor discretion is permitted?

Because much plagiarism may be inadvertent, instructors might believe that the most efficient solution in many cases is simply to have the student rewrite the paper, possibly with a lowered grade, and not report the instance. Even in an occasional case of deliberate cheating, the professor may believe that mitigating circumstances merit departure from institutional requirements. The institution will find it in its interest to establish guidelines that include the amount of discretion permitted and the circumstances that merit discretion. One student's discretion is another student's favoritism or discrimination. Therefore, policies should be in place to assure fairness.

➢ Is an instructor allowed not to report an instance of plagiarism?

➢ Is an instructor allowed to deviate from established policy, and if so, by what amount or under what circumstances?

➢ Is an instructor permitted to request a greater or a lesser penalty than policy dictates?

➢ Is there a difference in authority or discretion among teaching assistants, adjunct instructors, and regular faculty?

➢ Should the instructor confer with the department chair (or other person) before bringing a student in for a conference regarding suspected plagiarism?

6.2.5 Is a witness required during meetings with a student regarding plagiarism?

In the case of overt evidence, where mitigating facts are unlikely (as in the case of a student handing in a mill paper), it may be best to have a witness present, especially if the student is perceived as potentially troublesome. However, where plagiarism is only suspected, and where the goal may be confession, repentance, and rehabilitation, a witness may actually interfere with the process. This issue, then, is not necessarily easily resolved. What may turn out to be another case of ignorant and inadvertent plagiarism can be made terrifying and threatening by the presence of a department or divisional chair.

➢ Should the presence of a witness be required or be optional?

➢ If the presence of a witness is optional, whose choice should that be?

➤ Should the choice depend on set guidelines or be on a case-by-case basis?

6.2.6 Is there a statute of limitations?

Plagiarism may not be discovered during the term when the offending paper is handed in. Circumstances may occur that bring the cheating to light during the following term or even later. How long will the student be exposed to the risk of conviction?

➤ How long after a term ends can a student still be penalized for plagiarism committed during that term?

➤ If the plagiarism is discovered after the student graduates, can a penalty still be imposed (a note on the transcript, revocation of the degree, failure of the class with possible consequences relating to units needed for the degree, etc.)?

✓ 6.3 INSTITUTIONAL SUPPORT MECHANISMS.

Plagiarism is not merely an attempt to deceive a professor; it is an attempt to steal a degree from the institution. Therefore, the institution itself should provide support to professors for fighting this scourge. This section discusses some institution-wide mechanisms that might be implemented.

6.3.1 Consider an institutional honor code.

An honor code usually consists of a signed statement in which students promise not to cheat and not to tolerate those who do. Honor codes appear to have great success at some institutions (McCabe & Drinan, 1999), especially where there are shared values and culture (such as small private institutions or military academies), while their effectiveness has been questioned at other kinds of institutions (Maramark & Maline, 1993).

Appendix F, Section F.1 lists the URLs of the honor codes of several colleges and universities. There you will note that some honor codes are actually extensive statements of academic integrity, together with detailed policies and examples. Some institutions, such as Western Maryland College, require students to sign an honor pledge on each test or assignment, affirming that the honor code has been followed: "I have neither given nor received unauthorized aid on this piece of work, nor have I knowingly tolerated any violation of the Honor Code" (Western Maryland College, 2000).

6.3.2 Consider a reporting system to track offenders.

See whether or not you recognize this story. A faculty member brings a student in to discuss plagiarizing. The student eventually breaks down or cannot deny the fact because of the evidence but pleads for mercy on the basis of terrible extenuating circumstances and claims that this is the first time and that the event will never be repeated. The faculty member is merciful and reduces or even eliminates the penalty. After the term is over, the faculty member, in conversation with a member of another department on campus, learns that the student is widely known as a "cheating machine."

Repeat offenders demonstrate that they have not learned anything by being caught: They evidently believe that the risk of punishment is worth taking. If they indeed lack remorse and reformation, their punishments should be much harsher. It is therefore of value to an institution to keep a record of academic dishonesty and apply a sliding scale of punishment.

6.3.3 Consider implementing a special transcript grade for cheating.

At the University of Maryland, students convicted of cheating receive a grade of XF rather than an F on their transcripts (Maramark & Maline, 1993). Knowing that their academic transcripts will reflect a cheating penalty after a cheating conviction should provide a strong deterrent for students who may think in terms of tradeoffs and risks rather than ethics. Whereas plagiarizing may be worth the risk of an F on the assignment or even in the course, risking a cheating indication of the student's transcript may be another matter entirely.

Mechanisms should be established for the removal of the cheating indicator under certain circumstances or after a certain number of years.

6.3.4 Consider maintaining a local database of all papers turned in.

One method for reducing local copying is to require students to turn in their papers in electronic format and then add them to a database. Each paper can be checked for a match when it is turned in and then maintained in the database for future comparison. Comparison software can be developed in-house, or a commercial product such as Wordcheck can be used. (See Chapter 4, Section 4.6.5, for further information on this product.)

6.3.5 Contract with plagiarism screening company.

A plagiarism screening company, such as Plagiarism.org, maintains its own database of submitted papers from an institution, together with a database of papers from mill sites and other sources. (See Chapter 4, Section 4.6.1, for further information about this service.)

"Work? Well, I have 114 in the class,
so that's maybe 75 or 80 different
papers to grade."

✓ 6.4 DEVELOP SYSTEMATIC PENALTIES.

"Equal justice under law" might be the operative concept here. A range of penalties and rehabilitative remedies should be spelled out so that individual cases can be handled both fairly and systematically.

120

6.4.1 What are the penalties and how are they matched to the offense?

Instructors should be provided with a list of the possible penalties for plagiarism, together with guidelines for applying them according to the nature of the offense. The discussion involved in matching the penalty to the offense should be profitable for all faculty. Any consensus that could be reached would help standardize the processes and level the playing field for students, who should be taught a consistent set of rules. Here is a list of penalties, revealing the varying degrees of severity:

➢ a formal warning

➢ redo the assignment

➢ redo the assignment and get a lower grade on it

➢ an F on the assignment

➢ zero points for the assignment (equivalent to at least two Fs)

➢ a reprimand (letter in the student file)

➢ a course grade reduction

➢ an F in the course

➢ a cheating F in the course (such as XF on the student's transcript)

➢ academic probation

➢ lose privileges (e.g., holding an office in the Associated Students)

➢ lose all or part of academic scholarships

➢ be suspended from the institution

➢ be expelled from the institution

➢ a delay (such as a year) in the awarding of a degree

➢ revocation of a degree

In some cases, penalties may be combined, such as an F in the course and academic probation.

6.4.2 What are the possible rehabilitative remedies?

Many faculty are saddened at the thought that education is becoming an activity of crime and punishment. They dislike being police officers; many do not even enjoy grading, much less assessing penalties for academic dishonesty. Therefore, any opportunity to redeem or rehabilitate a wrongdoer will be welcomed. Here are some responses to plagiarism that may help improve the student while still not condoning the plagiarism:

➢ redo the assignment

➢ redo the assignment with additional annotations about process, respect for intellectual property, and carefulness of citation

➢ write a paper on plagiarism and cheating, including its ethical dimensions and the harm it causes various groups or individuals

➢ attend required counseling relating to academic integrity or personal ethics

➢ perform community service (e.g., teach about plagiarism)

✓ 6.5 ADMINISTRATIVE CONCERNS.

Institutional administrators can do much to support faculty in the battle against plagiarism. Establishing clear policies, providing training, and offering moral support will all aid in the effort. An additional benefit is that a set of clear, consistent, well-publicized and fairly enforced guidelines will help the institution avoid litigation over plagiarism charges and penalties.

6.5.1 Create a dialog for faculty consensus.

Uniform definitions and uniform penalties would be the ideal for an institution so that students will always know the rules and how to observe them. To gain such uniformity, administrators must bring faculty together to discuss the issues. What may appear straightforward when thinking about the ethics of buying a paper on-line can become much less clear when other forms of plagiarism are discussed. For example, Rebecca Moore Howard (1999) argues that

> there is, in fact, a category of positive plagiarism for students.... That category would be "patchwriting"—"copying from a source text and then deleting some words, altering grammatical structures, or plugging in one-for-one synonym-substitutes" (p. 89).

To prohibit students from engaging in this process, Howard says, is to perpetuate an "intellectual hierarchy." On the other hand, Edward M. White (1999) argues, "Someone who will not, or cannot, distinguish his or her ideas from those of others, or trace the origins of those ideas, offends the most basic principles of learning" (p. 210). Clearly, a dialog needs to take place where faculty can discuss these varying viewpoints and attempt to arrive at a consensus.

6.5.2 Develop or revise policy.

Different schools or departments may require variations in their approaches to the use of data, the kind and extent of collaboration, or the definition of common knowledge, and over time even general approaches may need updating to include changes in pedagogical technique (such as the use of collaborative writing or team case studies) and new technologies (such as appropriate use and citation of the Internet and electronic databases, or a student's duty to protect electronic files). Therefore, a single, fixed policy may not be achievable. But an institution should go as far as it can toward a standardized approach because such an approach is easier to manage, understand, apply, and follow. Appendix A provides several standard paragraphs and statements that can be used or modified as needed to support the creation of clear definitions and policies.

6.5.3 Publicize all policies.

Policies, rules, definitions, penalties, and administrative procedures (including appeal steps) should be publicly and easily available to administrators, department heads, faculty, adjuncts, teaching assistants, students (including graduate students), and even parents of undergraduates. Dissemination mechanisms might include printed handbooks, university catalogs, and Web sites (with links across the site to make the material highly visible and easily available). Students might be sent one or more e-mail messages summarizing this information and calling their attention to the locations of the full-text versions.

6.5.4 Train the faculty.

A series of faculty development sessions to inform faculty of policies and procedures would be helpful. At such a meeting, faculty can be given printed copies of all relevant information. Training related to the material in this handbook will also enable faculty to perform their multiple roles of education, prevention, identification, and discipline relating to plagiarism. Giving each member of the institution a copy of this handbook would provide them with tools and ideas appropriate to these roles, as well as some materials useful for teaching students about plagiarism.

6.5.5 Train the support staff.

Writing Center workers, tutors, librarians, and others whose function it is to support student learning also need training. The training should be in two areas. First, those who help students with their writing should be clearly informed about the degree of assistance allowed. Clear examples of permissible and impermissible help should be offered and printed as a resource. Second, staffers can be trained to watch for signs of plagiarism in student work. Librarians can exercise vigilance as they help or observe students going about research-paper related work, and tutors or Writing Center staff can learn to detect some of the signs of copying. Administrators should make clear to the staff by letter or meetings how seriously plagiarism is viewed by the university.

6.5.6 Employ a plagiarism specialist.

As mentioned briefly in Chapter 4, Section 4.5, an effective way to help combat plagiarism is to hire a specialist research librarian or other staff member to assist faculty in searching for sources of plagiarized papers. Such a position would provide both practical and symbolic advantage. As a practical matter, the researcher would, through experience, become an efficient expert in finding sources, and faculty members would be more likely to challenge papers if they knew someone else would search for the sources, saving the instructor many hours of time. Symbolically, this specialist would represent serious administrative support for academic integrity and would therefore encourage faculty members to report suspected cheating, knowing that they would not be fighting the battle alone. The position might also provide a deterrent effect for students, who would see it as a warning that the institution is not looking the other way while they cheat.

✓ 6.6 INSTRUCTOR CONCERNS.

As the "administrator" of your courses, you should work to make sure that rules and instruction regarding plagiarism are clear, systematic, and publicized to your students. Just a paragraph in a syllabus may not be enough.

6.6.1 Teach students to recognize and avoid plagiarism.

Student ignorance over what constitutes plagiarism was mentioned in Chapter 1, while Chapter 2 covered a number of training issues. Appendix B provides some instructional quizzes, and Appendix C provides examples of proper and improper uses of sources. Discussing these in class should help students understand the practical issues.

6.6.2 Inform students about protecting their intellectual property.

Because some paper sites on the Web require students to submit a paper in order to download one, and because a paper can also be sold or traded locally, any paper is now a valuable commodity. For this reason, students should be told to protect their papers and disks from theft. (Similarly, you should not put graded papers out in a pile for students to pick up.)

"Oh, no! That paper I just turned in is being recalled by the mill! All of the dates are off by 200 years!"

6.6.3 Consider a class honor code.

If your institution does not have an honor code, you still might consider instituting one for one or more of your classes. Students can be asked to sign a statement affirming that they will neither cheat nor tolerate those who do. (Check with an appropriate administrator for guidance before proceeding.) See Appendix A, Section A.3, for sample language, and Chapter 3, Section 3.3.4, for a related discussion of integrity statements.

6.6.4 Make your personal policies clear.

Your syllabus should clearly prohibit plagiarism, defining it and indicating penalties for it. The syllabus is not a substitute for classroom training, but it will put where you stand on record at the beginning of the term.

✓ 6.7 STUDENT CONCERNS.

It is only fair to students that they be fully informed about the expectations placed on them. As a part of the discussion of their role at the university, they might be presented with relevant information aimed at helping to prevent plagiarism. This may be done by informing them that all students are expected to observe the following standards of behavior:

➢ Be serious about learning and the educational enterprise, and do not attempt to take shortcuts around assignments.

➢ Exercise personal integrity in coursework, performing all assignments with the intention of honesty.

➢ Take careful notes when researching, in order to be sure always to separate the words and ideas of others from your own.

➢ Cite the use of each source, whether the information from the source is presented by quotation, paraphrase, summary, or mere allusion.

➢ When in doubt, ask for permission, clarification, or instruction.

As has been mentioned in the earlier chapters of this book, most if not all students will benefit from clear, example-filled instruction about plagiarism and the proper use of sources. If your institution offers a University 101 type of introduction to college course to freshmen, such a venue would be ideal for assuring that all incoming students are aware of the rules and practices for proper source use. Publishing practical material (guidelines, examples of both proper and improper source use) in the student handbook, in addition to the list of penalties, would prove helpful as well.

Notes:

Appendix A

Sample Definitions of Plagiarism and Policy Language

Taking something from one man and making it worse is plagiarism.

— George Moore (1852–1933)

Many institutional policies relating to plagiarism will need to be highly customized because the fine points of appeals processes or the specific hierarchy of penalties will vary so much from institution to institution (or even from department to department). On the other hand, definitions and general policies lend themselves to more generic use. This appendix offers several sample definitions and policy statements (written expressly for this book) that may be used either as they are or as thinking stimuli for the drafting of more suitable language. All statements have been kept brief so that they will be suitable for instructors' syllabi as well as for institutional handbooks. A number of examples of actual policy statements can be found by following the links listed in Appendix F.

✓ A.1 Definitions.

Institutions may want to determine whether a single definition of plagiarism will be both broad and specific enough to apply adequately to all the disciplines. The use of data, the permissibility of collaboration, requirements for citation, and even what constitutes common knowledge may differ from field to field, making a single definition a challenge. This section contains some sample definitions, ranging from the short and general to the more elaborate.

Example A.1.1

Plagiarism is the failure to distinguish the student's own words and ideas from those of a source the student has consulted. Ideas derived from another, whether presented as exact words, a paraphrase, a summary, or quoted phrase, must always be appropriately referenced to the source, whether the source is printed, electronic, or spoken. Whenever exact words are used, quotation marks or an indented block indicator of a quotation must be used, together with the proper citation in a style required by the professor.

Example A.1.2

Plagiarism involves taking someone else's work and claiming it as one's own. The work taken may be words, laboratory data, a computer program, a physical model or mock-up, a chemical sample or result, a photograph, a table, a graph, or other work.

Example A.1.3

Students are responsible for using the appropriate styles of citation of source material incorporated into their work. Ignorance of proper methods or specific applications of the rules of citation will not be accepted as an excuse for plagiarism. If there is any doubt about whether or how to cite a source, the student should consult the instructor or visit the Writing Center.

Example A.1.4

Plagiarism is pretending that an idea is yours when in fact you found it in a source. You can therefore be guilty of plagiarism even if you thoroughly rewrite the source's words. One of the goals of education is to help you work with and credit the ideas of others. When you use another's idea, whether from a book, a lecture, a Web page, a friend's paper, or any other source, and whether you quote the words or restate the idea in your own words, you must give that person credit with a citation. No source may elect not to be cited.

Example A.1.5

The purposes of education include learning how to think, how to write, and how to work with ideas. Copying or paraphrasing the words of others without attribution circumvents these purposes, and prevents a substantial portion of education from taking place. Those who copy work from others and submit it as their own are, in effect, saying that they do not really care to get an education but are content with counterfeiting it. The willing plagiarist is essentially a con artist and will be treated by the academy accordingly.

Example A.1.6

Plagiarism is the failure to cite sources properly. You may have cited your source, but if you do an improper or inadequate job of it, you can still be guilty of plagiarism. It is therefore crucial that you understand how to cite. The rules are not complicated. (1) For exact words, use quotation marks or a block indentation, together with the citation. (2) For a summary or paraphrase, show exactly where the source begins and exactly where it ends: Introduce the borrowing with a comment about it and close it with the citation.

Example A.1.7

Both as a student and later on in your career you will be constructing "information products" from your own unique materials and materials from others. A cardinal rule for knowledge workers is to honor the words and ideas of others by giving them credit whenever you make use of them. Not to do so is to steal their ideas, which is a good definition of plagiarism.

"I meant to put all those paragraphs in quotation marks, but the quote key on my keyboard is broken."

✓ A.2 POLICIES.

This section includes example language for several policies relating to plagiarism. While much of the language here spells out prohibitions, acceptable practices should also be mentioned, especially if they are normally not allowed at other institutions. (Self-recycling would be an example.) The framework of "rights and responsibilities" is a good one for constructing institutional policy because all constituencies can see what is allowed and what is not.

A.2.1 Multiple submission and self-recycling.

The permissibility of a student's reuse of written work should receive particular attention because many students are confused over the issue, and uniform policies are frequently missing.

Example A.2.1.1

Every written assignment must be completely new and original. Students are explicitly prohibited from submitting the same writing or portions of writing to more than one course. Similarly, no paper or other assignment prepared for another institution or for any other purpose may be submitted to a course at the university without the written permission of the professor. (For example, a professor may include on a syllabus a requirement for the student to bring in previously written creative work for analysis or revision.)

Example A.2.1.2

Because the purpose of writing assignments is to provide students with the opportunity to exercise fresh thinking and practice writing skills, all writing assignments must be fulfilled with completely new writing. Self-recycling, the use of the student's previous work in whole or in part, is not permitted.

A.2.2 Collaboration.

The regulation of collaboration may best be left to individual departments or even individual instructors since practice varies so widely.

Example A.2.2.1

The extent of permissible collaboration on writing or research projects should be clearly defined by the syllabi of individual courses. In some courses, students may be permitted to engage in and use joint research, edit, or even write a paper together. In the absence of clear permission to do so, however, each student is expected to do individual research and writing. It is always expressly prohibited for students to write a paper together and submit multiple copies of it to different professors or for different courses.

Example A.2.2.2

Collaboration for the purposes of this course may include the sharing of research sources (book titles, URLs, journal articles, and so forth), brainstorming and sharing of ideas, and peer editing of drafts. Collaboration in this course shall not include writing sections of a draft for another student, writing a paper together, or lending an electronic copy of a paper or draft to another student.

Example A.2.2.3

In this course, you will be writing your case study in groups of four to five. You may elect to have each group member write a separate section of the case or you may work in complete collaboration, perhaps identifying a researcher, a writer, an editor, and so on.

A.2.3 Individual responsibility.

Students sometimes prefer to shift the blame for breaches of academic integrity. A useful part of academic policy, then, is to remind them that they bear ultimate responsibility for their written products.

Example A.2.3.1

As with many other papers you turn in, you place your name prominently on the front as the writer. This act has several implications. First, it declares that you are the true author of all the words in the paper, except those that you have clearly indicated as quotations. Second, you assert that your ideas are presented within, and that when you have built upon the ideas of others, you have honored them with due credit in a citation. And finally, you take full responsibility for the accuracy of the text. The implication is that you have proofread the paper carefully and that every mark—present or absent—represents your intention.

Example A.2.3.2

Before you hand in your final paper, be sure to proofread it carefully. Whether you had the assistance of a typist, tutor, editor, professor, or writing center, you are fully and ultimately responsible for the paper's content and accuracy. Take extra care to be sure that the paper matches your intentions. For example, are there quotation marks everywhere there should be? Have you clearly marked each summary or paraphrase with an introductory tag and a closing citation?

A.2.4 Responsibility to protect writings.

Papers are being stolen and copied or sold all too often, especially now that doing so is merely a matter of a file copy or an e-mail attachment. Students should be warned to be careful with their own intellectual property as well as that of others.

Example A.2.4.1

You are expected to exercise reasonable care to protect your writings, in both printed and electronic form. Do not lend your papers to another for "reference." This process results in many papers being copied and turned in under the copyist's name or even uploaded to paper mill sites in trade for other papers. Such plagiarism may implicate you as an accessory or result in your being accused of plagiarism. If you know or believe your work has been stolen or copied, contact your professor immediately. If the term has ended, register a written complaint with the Office of the Academic Dean as soon as you are aware of the theft.

Example A.2.4.2

It is very important that you keep all drafts and materials used during the writing of your paper and that you guard your paper carefully in every form (printed or electronic). You may not upload your paper to a paper mill site, nor permit anyone else to upload it. Should a copy of your paper be lost or stolen, you should inform the professor immediately and be prepared to present your drafts and research materials as evidence of your true authorship. This caution is to protect you in the event your paper turns up on a paper mill site.

✓ A.3 HONOR CODES.

Honor codes can be simple or elaborate. The simplest is a statement by the student promising not to cheat and to report those who do.

Example A.3.1

This is an academic community where all students promise to exhibit personal integrity and honest behavior. The honor code exists to show trust for the student, to provide a fair environment for all, and to aid in the formation of character. Being a person of honor, neither cheating nor tolerating those who do, is one of the important goals of your education.

Example A.3.2

By signing the honor pledge, you promise to be on your best ethical behavior in all your work. You agree that you will not cheat on exams, not allow others to cheat from your work, nor tolerate the cheating of others if you witness it. On papers you will do your own work, not copying from other writers without attribution, not allowing others to copy your work, and not allowing others to write work for you.

Appendix B

Quizzes and Activities

This appendix contains several quizzes and other activities designed to be used in class to help determine students' knowledge of plagiarism and educate them about some of the specifics of citation. The quizzes are intended as teaching rather than evaluative tools; they will be used best to stimulate discussion about the topics, viewpoints, and varied answers. As appropriate, institutional policy and the generally accepted rules of source use and citation should be brought into the discussion.

✓ B.1 PLAGIARISM ATTITUDE SCALE.

On this personal opinion scale, there are no necessarily right or wrong answers. The survey can be used as a pedagogical tool to discuss student responses and how those responses correlate or conflict with institutional policy. Discovering why students feel the way they do may uncover unspoken misunderstandings or past perceived wrongs that can be aired and perhaps resolved in a positive direction.

Classroom testing of the survey revealed some interesting information. For example, freshmen were much less likely than sophomores, juniors, and seniors to agree with Statement 7, "If a student buys or downloads free a whole research paper and turns it in unchanged with his or her name as the author, the student should be expelled from the university." Most interesting was the fact that while most students agreed or strongly agreed with Statement 8,

"Plagiarism is against my ethical values," they also agreed with Statement 10, "It's okay to use something you have written in the past to fulfill a new assignment because you can't plagiarize yourself." Such a correlation may indicate that most students who engage in self-recycling do not do so with a mind to cheat, but because they believe it is legitimate. Since most institutions prohibit self-recycling, the issue becomes one of education rather than one of intentional disregard for the rules.

Small classes may profit from an informal discussion of the answers, while large classes might fill out the scale, have the answers tabulated, and at a future meeting see the results, combined with commentary from the professor. If you have statistical software, you may choose to conduct a more sophisticated analysis on the results to identify further points for discussion.

For your convenience in photocopying this scale, it is reproduced separately on the next two pages of this book. Before making photocopies, please read the copyright notice on page *ii* of this book, which describes your limited permission to make copies.

✓ B.2 CITATION QUIZ.

This quiz can be used to determine how accurately students are able to differentiate between material that requires a citation and material that does not. It might be given early in the term so that the results can be used to determine how much training the class needs and what specific areas involve the most uncertainty or confusion. Answers with explanations are given at the end of the quiz.

For your convenience in photocopying this quiz, it is reproduced separately on page 143. Before making photocopies, please read the copyright notice on page *ii* of this book, which describes your limited permission to make copies.

Plagiarism Attitude Scale

Directions: This is an attitude scale, which measures how you feel about plagiarism. It is *not* a test with right and wrong answers. Please consider your honest opinions regarding the items and record your responses. Do *not* place your name on this scale. Your instructor may give you further instructions.

1. Sometimes I feel tempted to plagiarize because so many other students are doing it.

   ☐ Strongly Agree ☐ Agree ☐ Neutral ☐ Disagree ☐ Strongly Disagree

2. I believe I know accurately what constitutes plagiarism and what does not.

   ☐ Strongly Agree ☐ Agree ☐ Neutral ☐ Disagree ☐ Strongly Disagree

3. Plagiarism is as bad as stealing the final exam ahead of time and memorizing the answers.

   ☐ Strongly Agree ☐ Agree ☐ Neutral ☐ Disagree ☐ Strongly Disagree

4. If my roommate gives me permission to use his or her paper for one of my classes, I don't think there is anything wrong with doing that.

   ☐ Strongly Agree ☐ Agree ☐ Neutral ☐ Disagree ☐ Strongly Disagree

5. Plagiarism is justified if the professor assigns too much work in the course.

   ☐ Strongly Agree ☐ Agree ☐ Neutral ☐ Disagree ☐ Strongly Disagree

6. The punishment for plagiarism in college should be light because we are young people just learning the ropes.

   ☐ Strongly Agree ☐ Agree ☐ Neutral ☐ Disagree ☐ Strongly Disagree

7. If a student buys or downloads free a whole research paper and turns it in unchanged with his or her name as the author, the student should be expelled from the university.

   ☐ Strongly Agree ☐ Agree ☐ Neutral ☐ Disagree ☐ Strongly Disagree

Continued on the next page. →

Plagiarism Attitude Scale (continued)

8. Plagiarism is against my ethical values.

   ☐ Strongly Agree ☐ Agree ☐ Neutral ☐ Disagree ☐ Strongly Disagree

9. Because plagiarism involves taking another person's words and not his or her material goods, plagiarism is no big deal.

   ☐ Strongly Agree ☐ Agree ☐ Neutral ☐ Disagree ☐ Strongly Disagree

10. It's okay to use something you have written in the past to fulfill a new assignment because you can't plagiarize yourself.

    ☐ Strongly Agree ☐ Agree ☐ Neutral ☐ Disagree ☐ Strongly Disagree

11. If I lend a paper to another student to look at, and then that student turns it in as his or her own and is caught, I should not be punished also.

    ☐ Strongly Agree ☐ Agree ☐ Neutral ☐ Disagree ☐ Strongly Disagree

12. If students caught plagiarizing received a special grade for cheating (such as an XF) on their permanent transcript, that policy would deter many from plagiarizing.

    ☐ Strongly Agree ☐ Agree ☐ Neutral ☐ Disagree ☐ Strongly Disagree

Citation Quiz

Directions: In each case, decide whether you must include a citation of the source for the information described.

1. In an article, you find the phrase "cultural tapeworm." You decide to use the phrase in your paper.
   □ have to cite it   □ do not have to cite it

2. You quote from an interview with your mother, who is an expert in the area about which you are writing.
   □ have to cite it   □ do not have to cite it

3. You read in several places about how popular fax machines are in both offices and homes. You mention in your paper that fax machines seem to be everywhere today.
   □ have to cite it   □ do not have to cite it

4. You do a survey of students on campus, asking about their musical preferences for the campus radio station. You report on the findings in your paper.
   □ have to cite it   □ do not have to cite it

5. In your paper, you write, "Abraham Lincoln grew up in a log cabin without electricity." This is a fact you have read many times in the past and you now do not remember where.
   □ have to cite it   □ do not have to cite it

6. In your paper, you summarize but do not quote a state court opinion, which is in the public domain (that is, not copyrighted).
   □ have to cite it   □ do not have to cite it

7. You decide to end your paper with a bit of wit and quote the proverb, "He who laughs last, laughs best."
   □ have to cite it   □ do not have to cite it

8. You are writing a paper on the effects of wildfires. On a Web page, you locate a photograph of the fires at Mesa Verde National Park and paste it into your paper.
   □ have to cite it   □ do not have to cite it

9. During one of his regular class lectures, your professor refers to the latest and still unpublished results of his experiments. You decide to mention these results in your paper for another class.
   □ have to cite it   □ do not have to cite it

10. You locate a brilliant argument in favor of an idea you are advancing in a paper. You decide to use this argument but turn it completely into your own words.
    □ have to cite it   □ do not have to cite it

Answers to the Citation Quiz on the Previous Page

1. Have to cite it. An apt or unusual phrase borrowed from another writer or speaker must be cited, even if it is only two words. In this case, the two words constitute a provocative metaphor. The creator of the phrase should be cited.

2. Have to cite it. Citing an interview is not any different from citing an article. Whenever you quote someone else's words—printed, spoken, or even sung—you must cite them. The fact that the interviewee is a relative is not relevant.

3. Do not have to cite it. This information would be considered common knowledge, found or known everywhere.

4. Do not have to cite it. When you do original research, you do not cite yourself if the research is conducted for the paper. (If you already published the research elsewhere, you would then need to cite yourself.)

5. Do not have to cite it. This is common knowledge, found in many sources.

6. Have to cite it. When you refer to a source, whether by quotation, summary, or paraphrase, you must cite it. That this usage involves a summary, a government document, and possibly a document that is not copyrighted is irrelevant to the need for citation.

7. Do not have to cite it. Proverbs are merely a specific type of common knowledge.

8. Have to cite it. Photographs and drawings are forms of ideas and have creators just as do words. Therefore, you must cite the source of the photograph.

9. Have to cite it. This information is unique (and therefore not common knowledge), so it must be cited. The fact that it is unpublished is irrelevant.

10. Have to cite it. Once again, the rule is, when you use another's words or ideas in the form of a quotation, a summary, *or a paraphrase*, you must cite the source. Turning someone else's ideas into your own words does not make the idea come from you. It still has a source that must be referenced.

✓ B.3 USING SOURCES QUIZ.

This activity consists of a true-false quiz about citation requirements. The quiz covers the same concepts as the Citation Quiz above, but in a more general or theoretical way. It might be used as a posttest after training. On the other hand, it can be given early in the semester to determine how much instruction about plagiarism is needed. A third possible use is as a stimulus for classroom discussion of the issue. Answers with explanations are given at the end of the quiz.

Using Sources Quiz

Directions: For each item, make a check mark to indicate whether it is true or false.

1. As long as you put another person's words into your own words, you don't need to cite the other person.
   ☐ True   ☐ False

2. As long as you put the author's name at the end of the paragraph, it is permissible to quote the author, even if you do not use quotation marks or a block indented quotation.
   ☐ True   ☐ False

3. Even if you do not quote, you must cite the use of an idea you found during your research.
   ☐ True   ☐ False

4. If you copy a paragraph from an old work that is no longer copyrighted, you do not have to cite it because it is in the public domain.
   ☐ True   ☐ False

5. Anything posted on the Web is common knowledge and can be used without citation.
   ☐ True   ☐ False

6. Even if what you are quoting is common knowledge (which normally needs no citation), you must cite the quotation because you used someone's exact words.
   ☐ True   ☐ False

7. If you locate a statement that very accurately reflects your own idea, then you can use it without quotation marks or citation.
   ☐ True   ☐ False

8. When you condense a large section of text into a summary, the summary becomes common knowledge and hence need not be cited.
   ☐ True   ☐ False

9. Plagiarism is the academic name for copyright infringement.
   ☐ True   ☐ False

10. It is possible to plagiarize by accident as well as by intention.
    ☐ True   ☐ False

Answers to the Using Sources Quiz on the Previous Page

1. False. Whenever you use another person's words *or* ideas, you must cite the source. Putting the ideas into your own words does not change the fact that you have gotten the ideas from another person.
2. False. Every quoted word must be either enclosed in quotation marks or set off from the main text as an indented block quotation, in addition to having the appropriate citation.
3. True. Ideas from sources need attribution, whether the ideas are quoted, summarized, paraphrased, or merely referred to.
4. False. You cite the source of all borrowed words or ideas. The issue of whether the words or ideas are copyrighted is irrelevant to citation issues. If you quote Aristotle, cite Aristotle.
5. False. Much of the information on the Web is unusual, or unique knowledge and must be cited. Any exact words you use from the Web must be quoted (quotation marks or block indent) and cited, even if they state common knowledge.
6. True. A quotation of any kind must be cited. If you quote a source saying, "The sun shines at noon," you must cite that source. Both ideas *and* words need attribution.
7. False. If you quote, you cite. It does not matter if the words precisely express your idea. Your own idea in your own words does not need to be cited. Your idea in another's words does.
8. False. Common knowledge is not the same as a summary.
9. False. Copyright infringement is the act of reproducing copyrighted words, even if you do not claim to have written them. Plagiarism is the act of reproducing any words or ideas and claiming them as your own, even if they are not copyrighted.
10. True. Ignorance of the rules of quotation and citation is a common source of unintentional plagiarism. Reusing your own previously written words where that practice is prohibited is another source of unintentional plagiarism.

"Why does Buskin
wiggle his fingers
when he hands in
a paper?"

"Oh, those are
just the
quotation
marks."

✓ B.4 ACCEPTABLE USE VERSUS PLAGIARISM EXERCISE.

This exercise allows students to discuss whether plagiarism has been committed. An effective use of this exercise might be to make six overhead transparencies, each with the source text and one of the six uses. Read the passages to the students and solicit opinions and reasons to back the opinions. Take a vote to determine the general understanding. Then discuss with the class how each use relates to the source (for example, the copying of exact words involves plagiarism). Answers with explanations are given at the end of the exercise.

Acceptable Use Versus Plagiarism Exercise

Directions: The first paragraph presents *source material* (a paragraph from an academic journal) that a student wants to cite. Below the source material are six ways that the source material might be used. For each *potential use*, indicate whether the use is acceptable or constitutes plagiarism.

Source Material

To communicate effectively with other people, one must have a reasonably accurate idea of what they do and do not know that is pertinent to the communication. Treating people as though they have knowledge that they do not have can result in miscommunication and perhaps embarrassment. On the other hand, a fundamental rule of conversation, at least according to a Gricean view, is that one generally does not convey to others information that one can assume they already have (Grice, 1975). A speaker who overestimates what his or her listeners know may talk over their heads; one who underestimates their knowledge may, in the interest of being clear, be perceived as talking down to them. Both types of misjudgment work against effective and efficient communication (Nickerson, 1999, p. 737).

Potential Use 1

To communicate effectively, we must have a reasonably accurate idea of what our listeners do and do not know that is pertinent to the communication. Treating people as if they know something they do not can result in miscommunication and perhaps embarrassment. On the other hand, a foundational rule of conversation, at least according to a Gricean view, is that we usually do not convey to others information that we can assume they already have (Grice, 1975). A speaker who overestimates what his or her listeners know may talk over their heads, while someone who underestimates their knowledge may be perceived as talking down to them. Both mistakes work against effective and efficient communication (Nickerson, 1999, p. 737).

☐ acceptable use   ☐ plagiarism

Potential Use 2

For effective communication, it is necessary to have a fairly accurate idea of what our listeners know or do not know that is pertinent to the communication. If we assume that people know something they do not, then miscommunication and perhaps embarrassment may result. At the same time, a fundamental rule of conversation is that we should not convey information that we assume our listeners already have. If our assumption is wrong, we may talk over our listeners' heads, or possibly be perceived as talking down to them. Both errors work against effective and efficient communication (Nickerson, 1999, p. 737).

☐ acceptable use   ☐ plagiarism

Potential Use 3

Nickerson (1999) argues that effective communication depends on a generally accurate knowledge of what the audience knows that "is pertinent to the communication." If a speaker assumes too much knowledge about the subject, the audience will either misunderstand or be bewildered. However, assuming too little knowledge among those in the audience may cause them to feel patronized. In either case, the communication will be less successful than it could have been (p. 737).

☐ acceptable use   ☐ plagiarism

Potential Use 4

As Raymond Nickerson (1999) reminds us, "To communicate effectively with other people, one must have a reasonably accurate idea of what they do and do not know that is pertinent to the communication" (p. 737). If we treat people as if they have knowledge that they do not have, we can cause miscommunication and perhaps embarrassment. On the other hand, it is important not to convey to others information that we can assume they already have. A speaker who overestimates what his or her listeners know may talk over their heads, and one who underestimates their knowledge may be perceived as talking down to them. Both of these wrong estimations work against effective and efficient communication.

☐ acceptable use   ☐ plagiarism

Potential Use 5

We are informed by Nickerson (1999), "To communicate effectively with other people, one must have a reasonably accurate idea of what they do and do not know that is pertinent to the communication." It is crucial to assume neither too much nor too little knowledge of the subject by the audience, or the communication may be inhibited by either confusion or offense (p. 737).

☐ acceptable use   ☐ plagiarism

Potential Use 6

If we are to engage in effective communication, we must not talk down to our audience nor talk beyond their understanding. It is therefore very important that we have a generally accurate idea of what our audience knows about the subject.

☐ acceptable use   ☐ plagiarism

Answers to Acceptable Use Versus Plagiarism Exercise

Potential Use 1. Plagiarism. This passage is virtually a word-for-word copy (with only a few words changed here and there), yet there are no quotation marks or other indications that it is a quotation. The citation by itself is an inadequate indication of the source. Quoted words must always be marked as quoted. Changing a few words here and there does not change the fact that most of the words are quoted.

Potential Use 2. Plagiarism. This passage is an inadequate paraphrase of Nickerson, since the passage has many words and phrases that echo the source. Also note that, as in Potential Use 1 above, the passage does not have an opening tag to indicate where use of the source begins. A citation at the end of a paragraph is not sufficient to indicate what is being credited to the source.

Potential Use 3. Acceptable use. This passage is an acceptable summary of Nickerson's words, and where it uses an exact phrase, it puts the phrase in quotation marks. Note the opening tag, "Nickerson (1999) argues" to indicate the beginning of the use of the source.

Potential Use 4. Plagiarism. This passage begins with a properly quoted and cited passage, but then it continues with a lightly modified quotation of the subsequent words in Nickerson's passage. The implication to the reader is that the words and ideas following the cited quotation are the student's, when in fact they are still Nickerson's.

Potential Use 5. Acceptable use. This is an appropriate combination of quotation and summary, with the summary in the student's own words and the citation in the proper place. Note that the beginning tag, "We are informed by," and the concluding citation enclose the borrowed material completely.

Potential Use 6. Plagiarism. Even though the student here has not quoted the passage word for word, the ideas have been taken from the passage and not cited. The lack of citation of the source of the ideas is plagiarism.

✓ B.5 "YOU BE THE JUDGE" ACTIVITY.

This activity is designed to help identify and develop students' ethical values as well as get the class thinking about the wider context and consequences surrounding plagiarism. The situations can be discussed either in small groups (which later report back to the entire class) or in a general class discussion. Small groups of four are highly effective in providing interaction. Each circumstance can be discussed in ten or fifteen minutes. Each group might be asked to develop a one- or two-sentence response to the questions asked at the end, and these could be shared with the class as a whole. Your comments might include some focusing information about university rules or policy, after which the class might address any differences between class answers and university position.

"You Be the Judge" Activity

Directions: For each of the following circumstances, answer the questions that appear immediately below them. The questions ask for your reactions and opinions.

Circumstance 1.

You are taking an introductory course in psychology that is graded on the curve. A seven-page paper is due for the course, representing 30 percent of the final grade. One day in the dormitory, just after the paper has been turned in, you overhear a student telling another that he copied the paper from the Web and turned it in, feeling that it will get an "A" because it was taken from a well-respected journal.

Questions: What, if anything, do you do? You may want to discuss your options and then choose from among them. Why is your chosen option the best? If the course were not graded on the curve, would your choice of action differ? If so, why?

Circumstance 2.

Your group constitutes the student disciplinary board of the university. Before you is the case of a student who has been caught plagiarizing. The student turned in an essay entirely copied word for word from his roommate's essay. You have not been given the details about how large a part of the grade the essay was to have been, or whether the class is graded on a curve.

Question: What penalty should be assessed? The range open to you includes everything from no penalty to expulsion from the university.

Circumstance 3.

A friend says that she is confused about the assignment in a class you took last semester and asks to see the paper you wrote to get an idea about proper form and approach. You lend her your paper. Just after the term is over, while you are visiting her in her room, you notice a paper with her name on it and an "A–" grade. Another glance tells you that you are actually looking at your paper—your friend copied it and turned it in to the professor as hers.

Questions: How would you feel? What should you do?

Circumstance 4.

You overhear a student down the hall in your residence building asking others for ideas for a paper he is writing. Eventually, he gets to you and shows you a draft of his work. It does not take much of a look for you to see that this student is an extremely weak writer who cannot write a grammatical or coherent sentence. His skills are so far below college level that you believe his paper will fail. Later that day, you mention your concerns to a friend, who tells you, "Don't worry. His tutor will take care of it." Three weeks later you learn that the student received a "B" on the paper.

Questions: What is your reaction to this set of circumstances? What, if anything, would you do? What, if anything, would you say, and to whom would you say it?

Circumstance 5.

For a course you are taking, you have been assigned to research and write definitions for ten obscure terms. As you stand in line on the due date, turning in your definitions, the girl in front of you tells her friend, "I just couldn't find anything on number six, but my boyfriend is a graduate student and he knows about this stuff, so he wrote it for me."

Questions: Do you think this girl has committed plagiarism? What if she had said, "He helped me write it," rather than "He wrote it for me"? Would you feel differently about the situation if you had been unable to find any information about number six yourself? If you would feel differently, why?

Appendix C

Teaching Resources

They lard their lean books with the fat of others' works.

– Robert Burton (1576–1640)

This appendix contains several items suitable for overhead transparencies, together with some commentary that may be used to accompany the transparencies in a lesson to students. These materials are designed to reduce the amount of confusion among students over how to use sources appropriately.

✓ C.1 CITATION DECISION CHART 1: WHEN SHOULD YOU CITE?

Students often ask, "How do I know when to cite and when not to?" Chart 1 is a decision chart that shows, in simplified form, how to determine what needs to be cited and what does not.

C.1.1 Commentary for Chart 1.

The general goal of citation is to distinguish between the student's ideas and those of others. The first question, "Did you think of it?" might also be expressed as, "Is it yours?" Anything that you originated (thought of, created, discovered) does not need to be cited. A personal experiment, personal observation, your opinions, interpretations, judgments, ideas, thoughts, commentary, analysis, narrative, description, argument—whatever belongs to you does not need to be cited.

Similarly, whatever does *not* originate with you *does* need to be cited. Other people's experiments, personal observations, opinions, interpretations, judgments, ideas, thoughts, commentary, analysis, narrative, description, argument—whatever belongs to another person (or organization) does need to be cited.

There is one exception to this latter rule. Common knowledge does not need to be cited. Common knowledge includes whatever an educated person would be expected to know or could locate in an ordinary encyclopedia. For example:

➤ Easily observable information. (Heat makes people tired in summer; puppies display tremendous energy; the *Diagnostic and Statistical Manual* contains standard descriptions and diagnoses of mental conditions.)

➤ Commonly reported facts. (Poet George Herbert was born in 1593 and died in 1633; Napoleon's army was decimated by the winter march on Moscow during the War of 1812; grapefruit juice can potentiate some medications.)

➤ Common sayings. ("Waste not, want not"; "Look before you leap"; "He who hesitates is lost.")

There are some *cautions* to the above:

➤ While common knowledge need not be cited, *the specific expression of common knowledge must be identified*. For example, you may mention without citation, as above, that Napoleon's army suffered ruinous losses during the march on Moscow. However, if your source says, "Napoleon's army froze in droves as it struggled ever so futilely toward Moscow," you must use quotation marks and cite the source of those words if you include them. Therefore, if you use someone's words, you must quote and cite them, even if they contain an idea that is common knowledge.

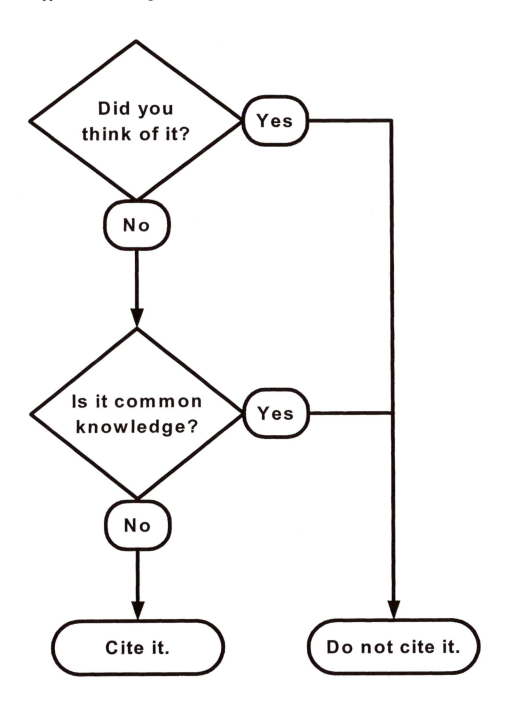

Citation Decision Chart 1: When should you cite?

➢ A fact or two of common knowledge taken from an encyclopedia need not be cited. However, you may not summarize or paraphrase long passages because the structure of information (its sequencing, emphasis, and selection) is not common knowledge and will need attribution.

➢ Common knowledge is often intermingled with interpretation, analysis, and opinion in many sources. All such commentary on common knowledge must be cited.

➢ You may not always know what is common knowledge. The rule here is, "If in doubt, cite it." It is much better to cite unnecessarily than to neglect citing something that should have been cited.

➢ Sometimes common knowledge sources disagree. General sources may differ about the dates of certain events, the number of people involved, or even the definition of a term. If you are aware of such disagreement, you should cite the source you use or use and cite both pieces of conflicting information.

Example C.1.1.1

Another urban legend states that Kentucky Fried Chicken changed its name to KFC because the company's product is now made from a genetically altered animal that cannot legally be called "chicken." This claim is refuted by a visit to any KFC restaurant, where multiple signs describe various "chicken" products.

The example above could have been written by a student who described the urban legend in his or her own words, thus requiring no citation because the legend is common knowledge and the refutation is easily observed. However, compare the previous example with this one:

Example C.1.1.2

Another urban legend states that Kentucky Fried Chicken changed its name to KFC because the company's product is now made from "genetically manipulated organisms" which are "kept alive by tubes" because they have "no beaks" to eat with. This claim is shown to be false because KFC "still uses the word 'chicken' ubiquitously in its advertising" and on its Web site.

A student writing the sentences in Example C.1.2 would need to cite the quotations even though they relate to common knowledge. The citation(s) would be needed to identify the exact quotations of source(s). (In this example, the source is Emery, 2000.)

✓ C.2 CITATION DECISION CHART 2: WHAT NEEDS TO BE CITED?

Chart 2 is another decision chart, this one making the point that using another's idea, even without using another's exact words, still requires a citation. Many students appear to believe that if they paraphrase or summarize a source, no citation is needed because they have made the idea "theirs" by turning it into their own words.

C.2.1 Commentary for Chart 2.

Chart 2 clearly distinguishes between "quote and cite" and "cite," as well as between "another's words" and "another's idea." This distinction should help students understand the obligation to cite *ideas* and not just words.

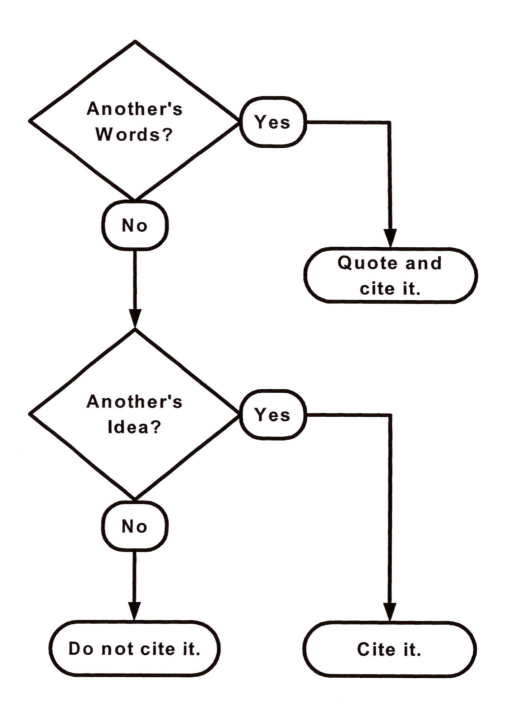

Citation Decision Chart 2: What needs to be cited?

"I should write my own papers more often.
I can't believe all the neat stuff I'm learning!"

✓ C.3 USING SOURCES: THE SIMPLE RULE.

The simple rule for using sources is "Mark the boundaries." This means that the words or idea used must have the beginning and the ending marked in some way. Chart 3 clarifies the rule.

The Simple Rule for Using Sources

→ Mark the Boundaries ←

For exact words
- phrase
- part of a sentence
- two or three sentences

**Boundaries are marked by
opening and closing quotation marks
and a citation.**

For a long quotation of exact words
- more than four lines
- paragraph
- two paragraphs

**Boundaries are marked by
a lead-in, a block indentation,
and a citation.**

When using a source but not quoting
- summarizing
- paraphrasing
- mentioning briefly
- using an idea from the source

**Boundaries are marked by
a lead-in and a close.**

Chart 3: The Simple Rule

C.3.1 Commentary for Chart 3.

In Modern Language Association (MLA) style, the close of the boundary is usually the citation (author's last name or short title and a page number), thus making easy the marking of the two boundaries. In American Psychological Association (APA) style, the citation is often included in the lead-in, as seen in many examples in this book, which follows APA style. Much student work will involve citing specific parts of studies, in which case the closing boundary (for both MLA and APA) will be a page number. However, when an entire study is cited, the entire citation may occur at the lead-in (for APA). In such cases, a close might involve the end of a paragraph or another indicator (such as a logical transition) that a new idea is being opened. See Example C.3.3.7 below for a possibility.

C.3.2 Other descriptions of the simple rule.

Students often conceptualize processes and strategies differently, and using a different term can sometimes bring clarity when another term fails to produce comprehension. You therefore might want to use some alternate ways to describe the simple rule. Among alternatives are these:

➤ framing the usage

➤ enclosing the borrowing

➤ fencing the borders

➤ circumscribing the usage

➤ differentiating your idea from a borrowed idea

➤ girdling the fat citation [humorous]

➤ bracketing the borrowing [alliterative]

C.3.3 Examples of the simple rule.

Here are several examples of the proper application of "mark the boundaries." (Note: References ascribed to John Doe are fictional; others are listed in the references at the end of the book.) The following example of quoting a phrase illustrates marking the boundaries with quotation marks and then adding the appropriate citation at the end.

Example C.3.3.1

One researcher refers to this phenomenon as an "encrypted personality" (Doe, 1997, p. 1414).

Quoting a part of a sentence involves the same technique as quoting a phrase. Note that in the next example the author is named to supply an additional opening boundary marker.

Example C.3.3.2

Christopher Ferguson (2000) says that for psychotherapists to deny the existence of free will may present problems for clients who wish to "rediscover free will and . . . rational choice" (p. 762).

Quoting one or more sentences is often better supported by a longer opening tag, in this case some summary information. The author is named in front of the summarized material to provide a beginning boundary, and the page number closes the boundary behind the quotation—as illustrated in the next example.

Example C.3.3.3

Arnett (2000) proposes a new period of development for ages 18-25, emerging adulthood: "Emerging adulthood is distinguished by relative independence from social roles and from normative expectations" (p. 469).

For quoting longer material, an indented block quotation is used. The quotation is introduced by a marker and closed by the citation (page number) as illustrated in the next example.

Example C.3.3.4

In emerging adulthood theory (Arnett, 2000), the period between ages 18 and 25 is one of exploration:

> Emerging adulthood is distinguished by relative independence from social roles and from normative expectations. Having left the dependency of childhood and adolescence, and having not yet entered the enduring responsibilities that are normative in adulthood, emerging adults often explore a variety of possible life directions in love, work, and worldviews. Emerging adulthood is a time of life when many different directions remain possible, when little about the future has been decided for certain, when the scope of independent exploration of life's possibilities is greater for most people than it will be at any other period of the life course. (p. 469)

For summarized material, the beginning of the summary is marked to set it off from the writer's own ideas. In the following example, the author's name is used as the beginning boundary marker, and the page number is the ending marker, so that the borrowed material is clearly marked off from the paper writer's own comments both before and after the use of the source.

Example C.3.3.5

The transition between childhood and adulthood is often described merely as adolescence—a long period bridging the two states. However, Arnett (2000) proposes a distinct period between adolescence and adulthood, which he names "emerging adulthood," a time of life in which incipient adults gain some but not full independence and examine the various options of life in both relationships and philosophies (p. 469). The traditional college student, therefore, is an emerging adult, exploring and testing the various choices of life before deciding which ones deserve long-term pursuit.

Even a mere brief reference to an author's idea should be set off by boundary markers, which again in this case are the idea's creator and the page number of the source as illustrated in the next example.

Example C.3.3.6

College freshmen, the typical eighteen-year-olds, are usually described as adolescents, although Arnett (2000) believes they have left that stage (p. 469).

Note that if you refer to an entire study rather than to a specific part of it, you can indicate the close of the reference through another means, such as the end of a paragraph, a logical transition, or a clearly direct response to the source. In the next example, there is a clear, logical transition from the source (Arnett) and the views of others.

Example C.3.3.7

In a recent paper, Arnett (2000) proposes an intermediate state between adolescence and adulthood. Traditional views, on the other hand, have viewed adolescence as a direct transition into adulthood.

✓ C.4 IMPROPER USE OF SOURCES.

Showing examples of inappropriate use of sources is another way to show students the proper way because bad examples can teach as well as good ones.

C.4.1 Neglecting to quote "just a couple of words."

Source C.4.1.1

As with a typical superhero, Judge Robertson thought it his duty not only to establish justice but to wreak equity. —Doe, 2000, p. 644

Paraphrase C.4.1.1

Judge Robertson felt duty-bound not only to labor for justice but to wreak equity (Doe, 2000, p. 644).

The paraphrase immediately above commits plagiarism because even though it cites the source, it copies the apt or unusual phrase "wreak equity" without quoting it. The simple remedy is to put the phrase in quotation marks.

C.4.2 Unacceptable paraphrase.

Source C.4.2.1

In a typical search strategy, Boolean operators can be used to control both the scope of the search and the required proximity of search terms. The operator OR expands the search by allowing the return of documents containing either search term, while the operator AND restricts the search by requiring both terms to be present in the document. Similarly, the proximity operator NEAR returns all documents in which the search terms are located within a set number of words of each other, while ADJ returns only documents in which the terms are next to each other (adjacent) in either order (Doe, 2000, p. 453).

Paraphrase C.4.2.1

When searching, you can use **Boolean operators to control the scope of the search and** how near each other the search terms are. For example, **the operator OR expands the search by** returning all **documents containing either search term**, while **AND restricts the search by requiring both terms to be present.** On the other hand, the use of NEAR will return **all documents in which the search terms are located within a** specific **number of words of each other**, while ADJ produces hits of pages where **the terms are adjacent** (Doe, 2000, p. 453).

The paraphrase immediately above omits several words and changes others, but it still contains many phrases (placed in boldface type for easy identification) which are copied word for word from the original, and therefore commits plagiarism. (Note also that it does not indicate the beginning of the paraphrase in order to distinguish it from the writer's own ideas. It thus violates the "mark the boundaries" rule.) Compare this to the following acceptable paraphrase:

Paraphrase C.4.2.2

According to John Doe (2000), using the appropriate forms of Boolean logic can allow the searcher to "control both the scope of the search and the required proximity of search terms." The word OR produces a hit (a matched document) when either term is present, while AND produces a hit only when both terms are matched in a document. It is also possible to locate documents where the search terms occur within a fixed number of words of each other (using NEAR) or when the terms are adjacent to each other (using ADJ), regardless of which term is first (p. 453).

In the paraphrase immediately above, the writer has carefully used different words and different sentence structures to reproduce the original writer's idea, and has marked the boundaries of the paraphrase by introducing the author at the beginning and then closing with the page number.

C.4.3 Unacceptable summary.

Source C.4.3.1

Recent experience reveals that the biodiversity of nature may be beneficial to disease resistance and crop productivity, an idea that runs counter to current agricultural practice of creating superstrains of various crops. In China, for example, rice yields more than doubled and the requirements for antifungal applications declined after the introduction of a second strain of rice in fields (Doe, 2000, p. 221).

Summary C.4.3.1

Contrary to the **current practice of creating superstrains**, mixing strains of crops together may increase **disease resistance and crop productivity**, as recent experience with rice in China shows (Doe, 2000, p. 221).

The above summary commits plagiarism by retaining exact phrases from the original text. Compare it to the following acceptable summary:

Summary C.4.3.2

In his science news column, Doe (2000) reports that farmers in China have doubled their yields and reduced the occurrence of disease by planting two strains of rice together, a fact now calling into question the common use of superstrain planting (p. 221).

Once again, in this acceptable summary, notice that the beginning of the summary is clearly marked by an introductory tag. Training students to provide these tags will go far to reduce the amount of confusion (on their part and on the instructor's) over what they see or claim as their own ideas and what they are attributing to a source.

✓ C.5 Plagiarism FAQ.

FAQ (pronounced *fack*) is an acronym for "frequently asked questions." Here is a list of questions students often ask about the issue of plagiarism:

C.5.1 What's the big deal about plagiarism anyway?

A major issue, of course, is academic integrity and the goal of education to help develop ethical, honest citizens who will not lie or steal. That point is made repeatedly in discussions of plagiarism, so you must be well aware of it. There is another issue, relating to your education, however, that is also important. Your professors want to help you learn how to work with ideas, as you take them and use them to build an argument or support your case. Can you find other sources? Can you use them effectively? In other words, are you preparing to become a competent and valuable knowledge worker?

C.5.2 What if I know some specific knowledge that isn't common knowledge?

You should cite it, if you know the source, or clearly state that it comes from personal experience. This is especially true if the knowledge involves numbers of any kind (data, statistics, counts) because they usually imply an experiment or measurement. Occasionally, when you look up a piece of specific knowledge, you may find that your memory of it is at variance with the published account. This situation reveals the benefit of checking and citing.

C.5.3 What's my motivation to be honest when everyone else is plagiarizing?

First, not everyone else is plagiarizing. An exact number is impossible to determine, and rates may vary widely from institution to institution or from course to course, but based on some samplings, the best guess is that the intentional plagiarism rate is less than ten percent. Your motivations to be honest include displaying academic integrity, building character, and learning by doing the assignment. Take your education seriously and appreciate the value of researched writing. Such assignments should not be seen merely as hurdles to jump over or obstacles to get by. Learn from them.

C.5.4 Why can't I use a paper I have already written?

The goal of a writing assignment is to enable you to learn. Defining a problem, locating sources, evaluating them, incorporating them into your thinking and writing, and coming to new knowledge and understanding—these are the goals of the assignment. The goal is not simply to plop a paper—any paper—on the professor's desk and then to check off the assignment.

Appendix D

Internet Search Tools

Plagiarists are always suspicious of being stolen from.

– Samuel Taylor Coleridge

This appendix lists search tools in a number of categories. These tools can be used to look for the on-line source of suspect texts, whether the source is a posted article on the Web, a paper from a paper mill, or an entry in an on-line reference work. Guidelines for choosing and using particular tools are provided under each tool type. The list is selective rather than exhaustive; individual tools have been chosen for their usefulness in the plagiarism detection process. Additional space is provided at the end of the appendix for noting search, reference, or content sites specific to your own discipline.

Note that these tools were active at the addresses listed at press time. Because of the nature of the Web, some URLs may have changed and some sites may have been closed down.

✓ D.1 SEARCH ENGINES.

A search engine consists of a large index of the content of Web pages that have been visited by the search engine's indexing software (called a spider or bot or robot). The larger search engines index every word on each Web page they visit, making them ideal

169

tools for finding copied paragraphs or even phrases. Suggestions for using a search engine include the following:

➢ Use several engines because each engine indexes a somewhat different portion of the Web, and no engine covers the Web completely.

➢ An exact-phrase search on a four- to six-word phrase from a paper will usually locate the paper instantly if the paper has been copied from the Web. (Many of the engines perform an exact-phrase search when the phrase is enclosed in quotation marks. See the help screens of individual engines for details.)

➢ Alternative to an exact-phrase search is to enter four to six keywords from the paper that as a group define its uniqueness. These words can be located anywhere in the paper. If an exact phrase search does not return the desired information, enter the same words as a keyword search (that is, the same phrase but without quotation marks).

Google
http://www.google.com
Google has one of the largest databases, with over a billion pages indexed. It now permits exact-phrase searches, and its method of arranging hits (pages that match the search criteria) usually brings the most relevant content to the beginning of the list.

Webtop
http://www.webtop.com
Webtop has indexed more than five hundred million pages, making it also one of the largest engines.

Fast
http://www.alltheweb.com
Fast also has a very large database, and, as its name implies, returns its hits quickly.

AltaVista
http://www.altavista.com
AltaVista has a large database and is a useful additional tool in any search. Exact-phrase searches are performed with quotation marks.

Northern Light
http://www.northernlight.com
Northern Light's database is a little smaller than those of the previous engines, but it is still large, and it often includes very recent pages. If you suspect your source may be a recent one, Northern Light is a good starting place. The search

engine allows exact-phrase searches by using quotation marks. Northern Light also includes a proprietary database of fee-based content.

HotBot
http://hotbot.lycos.com
Another of the large-database engines, HotBot is a good tool to include among the handful you use.

Excite
http://www.excite.com
Smaller but still in the hundreds of millions of pages, the Excite database is worth a look.

GoTo
http://www.goto.com
GoTo is a useful site for locating on-line commercial paper mills. If you want to find paper sales sites in addition to those listed in Appendix E, GoTo will provide a list. Search under "termpapers" or "research papers."

✓ D.2 METASEARCH TOOLS.

Dogpile
http://www.dogpile.com
Dogpile is a metasearch tool. It submits the user's query to several different search engines and reports the results of all those searches. Fast and well organized, Dogpile is recommended as a first-strike weapon for locating a paper on the Web.

Mamma
http://www.mamma.com
Mamma is another metasearch tool that saves the user from having to visit several search engines serially.

✓ D.3 DIRECTORIES.

Directories are the tools of choice for locating on-line material by topic or title rather than by phrase or keyword. If you have a paper on the complications caused by sleep apnea, you might want to use a directory to "drill down" from the general topic of health until you reach specific articles on sleep disturbance. The advantage directories have over search engines is that the sites listed are chosen and classified by humans, who include sites from the deep

Web as well as the visible Web. What a search engine's spider may miss, the human may have located and indexed in the directory. Because directories are humanly chosen, each is unique, and visiting several of them is a good strategy when searching for a suspect paper. Suggestions for using a directory include the following:

> Use the search function of the directory to perform a keyword search. This technique can save time over drilling down through the many levels of the directory.

> Drill down a step at a time to see what subject categories are available at each level. You may gain insight into how the paper you are seeking is categorized.

Yahoo
http://www.yahoo.com
Yahoo is the most famous directory, and it is also one of the largest, with more than two million sites listed. As with most directories, the user can "drill down" (move down from more general to more specific categories a step at a time), search the directory by keyword, or connect to a partner search engine (which changes from time to time).

Google Directory
http://directory.google.com
The Google Directory is based on the Open Directory Project, a directory created by many volunteer users and containing one of the three largest directory databases (over two million entries). Google's enhancement to the Open Directory is to use its unique ranking system for returning hits when the directory is searched.

LookSmart
http://www.looksmart.com
At more than two million entries, LookSmart is the third of the big three directories. It features an easy-to-use structure and well-chosen links.

✓ D.4 DEEP WEB SOURCES.

Here are several sites that feature links to deep Web databases, the databases that cannot be indexed by search engines but can be accessed directly by the user. They function much like directories, except that your search ends at a searchable database, such as a specialty encyclopedia or collection of government documents, rather than a single Web page.

InvisibleWeb.com
http://www.invisibleweb.com
Features more than ten thousand databases in a directory format that also has search capability.

CompletePlanet
http://www.completeplanet.com
Well-organized directory-style list of databases, including search capability.

WebData.com
http://www.webdata.com
Directory-style list of databases. The number of databases listed is smaller than that of Invisible Web or CompletePlanet, but there are many good links. Search capability.

FindArticles
http://www.findarticles.com
Full text of hundreds of journals.

MagPortal.com
http://www.magportal.com
Full text of magazine articles.

Deja.com
http://www.deja.com/usenet/
Deja.com provides searching of newsgroup postings.

✓ D.5 BOOK REVIEW SITES.

These sites provide book reviews, tables of contents, and in some cases, sample chapters. The information provided by a book review may be enough to identify a possible source of a suspect text. You can then locate a copy of the book in your library or through interlibrary loan and make a comparison. These sites will also be useful if you have assigned a book review as a writing project.

Bookspot Book Reviews
http://www.bookspot.com/bookreviews.htm
Bookspot contains all kinds of book information (such as reading lists, publishers' addresses, book news). The review page contains links to more than a dozen sites with book reviews.

Amazon.com
http://www.amazon.com
This well-known e-commerce site features thousands of book descriptions, reviews, tables of contents, and many sample chapters.

Barnes & Noble.com
http://www.bn.com
Read descriptions and reviews of many books.

***New York Times* Book Reviews**
http://www.nytimes.com/books
The *Times* features more than 50,000 lengthy book reviews in many subject areas.

✓ D.6 REFERENCE SITES.

These sites contain reference works or links to reference works, such as encyclopedias, almanacs, and dictionaries.

Encyclopedia Britannica
http://www.britannica.com

Xrefer
http://www.xrefer.com
Several reference works, such as literary encyclopedias.

Refdesk.com
http://www.refdesk.com
Directory site of many reference works (several encyclopedias, for example).

Biography.com
http://www.biography.com
Thousands of short biographies.

Bartleby.com
http://www.bartleby.com
Bartlett's quotations, literary handbooks, and other reference works.

✓ D.7 HOMEWORK HELPER SITES.

A number of sites on the Web function as directories to educational sites. By tracing a student's research process, you may find the source of a suspect text.

StudyWeb
http://www.studyweb.com

Education Index
http://www.educationindex.com

Education Planet
http://www.educationplanet.com

LibrarySpot
http://www.libraryspot.com

All Academic
http://www.allacademic.com

"You found my paper at FreePapers.com?! That's *impossible!* I paid good money for it from EssaySales, Inc.!"

✓ D.8 SEARCH ENGINES FOR ON-LINE PAPERS.

EssayCrawler
http://www.essaycrawler.com
This tool covers eleven free essay sites in addition to on-site essays. The site claims to search on a total of 35,000 essays.

Essay Find
http://www.freeessay.com/find/
This engine enables the user to search more than two dozen free essay sites, one at a time, by clicking on the site name.

Essay Finder
http://members.aol.com/oohalooo/essayfinder/index.html
This search engine covers several free paper sites and consolidates the results. Fast response.

Essay Search
http://http://www.essaysearch.com
This engine covers a few sites not searched by the tools above.

✓ D.9 SUBJECT NOTES SITES.

As with homework helper sites or even encyclopedias, the information at these sites certainly has legitimate use. However, because any electronic text is subject to abuse, the material here may also be stolen and plagiarized by unscrupulous students.

GiveMeNotes.com
http://www.givemenotes.com
Free lecture, book, and homework notes in a variety of subject areas, including business, computers, arts, language, government, history, literature, mathematics, music, physical education, religion, science, social science, and writing.

SparkNotes.com
http://www.sparknotes.com
Free articles, summaries, and lessons in several areas, including literature, history, health/nutrition, Shakespeare, poetry, biography, philosophy, psychology, economics, mathematics, biology, physics, chemistry, astronomy, computer science, and geography.

✓ D.10 LITERARY WORKS SITES.

Humanities courses (history, philosophy, literature especially) often include essays about literary works. Several Web sites cater to the "Cliff's Notes" crowd by offering summaries and analysis.

Awerty
http://www.awerty.com
Essay search, paper mill sites, and literary summaries are available free.

CheatBooks.com
http://www.cheatbooks.com
Niche bookstore (linked to Amazon.com) offering for sale Cliff's Notes, Barron's Book Notes, Max Notes, Bloom's Reviews, and Classics Illustrated Notes.

Classic Notes by GradeSaver
http://www.gradesaver.com/ClassicNotes/Titles
Notes for many standard literary works. The amount of material varies from book to book, but some books include biography, background, summary and analysis, and *interpretive essays ripe for downloading.*

FreeBooknotes.com
http://www.freebooknotes.com
Summaries and notes about literary works (mostly novels and plays).

Novelguide.com
http://www.novelguide.com
Summaries and interpretations of novels.

PinkMonkey.com
http://www.pinkmonkey.com
MonkeyNotes and Barron's Book Notes are available for literary works, together with study guides, test preparation, and so on. Free, but registration is required.

✓ D.11 SITES FOR YOUR DISCIPLINE.

Specific directories and sites for most disciplines can be found on the Web. Through experience and some research on the Web, you will be able to locate a number of promising avenues for locating suspect paragraphs or essays. As you locate them, use the spaces below to keep track.

Appendix D Internet Search Tools

Name: _____

URL: _____

Comment: _____

Name: _____

URL: _____

Comment: _____

Name: _____

URL: _____

Comment: _____

Name: _____

URL: _____

Comment: _____

Name: _____

URL: _____

Comment: _____

Appendix E

Term Paper Mills

This appendix lists Web sites that offer papers either free or for sale. The papers hosted by some of the free sites can be located with a search engine. For other free sites and for all of the fee-based sites, you will need to visit the site itself to see whether a copy of a suspect paper is located there. This list provides you with the Web addresses of many sites.

The free sites will allow you to download the entire text of a paper, and you will then be able to compare it with your suspect one directly. For the fee-based sites, you will need to compare the description of the paper on the site with the paper in your hand. Some sites, such as those operated by The Paper Store (see Section E.4), offer detailed descriptions that may allow you to make a very probable match.

This list is not intended to be exhaustive, but includes most of the major sites, together with many smaller sites. Even during the process of collecting this list, several sites disappeared and a few others appeared. Thus, while this list was current at press time, you will most likely discover that some of the URLs no longer work or have been redirected to other sites (some of which may no longer be in the paper mill arena). Some of the free sites appear to be run by students who may lose interest after awhile. If you want to update this list, you can use a search engine. Searching on "term papers," "termpapers," "research papers," "free term papers," "free research papers," "college essays," "essays free," and the like will bring you the appropriate results. (Note that at most sites the terms "paper," "essay," "research paper," and "term paper" are all used loosely and interchangeably.)

Note: For a list of search engines dedicated to locating essays, see Appendix D, Section D.8.

✓ E.1 SITES LISTING TERM PAPER MILLS.

Many free mill sites include links to other sites or to lists of "top sites," often called top 25, 50, or 100 sites, though the lists are seldom that lengthy. However, once you get to one site, you will have no trouble getting to many others.

Essay Find
http://www.freeessay.com/find
Search engine for about two dozen paper sites.

Essay Link Database
http://www.essaylinks.cjb.net

FreeEssay.com
http://www.freeessay.com
A portal for more than a dozen free paper sites. (See E.2 below for a list.)

Term Paper Sites
http://www.termpapersites.com
Access to 60,000 papers.

United Paper Database
http://www.updatabase.com
http://essays.virtualave.net
Combined databases from several free paper sites.

✓ E.2 SITES LINKED TO FREEESSAY.COM.

Freeessay.com is a portal for a dozen free paper sites, as well as a search engine for free papers from about two dozen sites.

A+ Papers
http://www.freeessay.com/aplus

AP Papers
http://www.freeessay.com/ap

Creative Essays
http://www.freeessay.com/creative

Essays Galore
http://www.freeessay.com/galore

EZ Essays
http://www.freeessay.com/ez

Hot Essays and Papers
http://www.freeessay.com/hot

Instant Essays
http://www.freeessay.com/instant

Joe's Essays
http://www.freeessay.com/joe

Killer Essays
http://www.freeessay.com/killer

Smart Essays
http://www.freeessay.com/smart

Student Essays
http://www.freeessay.com/student

Student Papers
http://www.freeessay.com/papers

✔ E.3 OTHER SITES WITH FREE PAPERS.

Paper mill sites offering free papers allow easy access to them, so that you can locate the full text of papers on the subject of your suspect paper and compare them.

123HelpMe.com
http://www.123helpme.com
40,000 papers, both free and for sale.

123student.com
http://www.123student.com
1,000 free papers.

Absolutely Free Online Essays
http://www.essays.terrashare.com/papers.html
Also known as The Student Essay Network.

BigNerds.com
http://www.bignerds.com
Free papers.

Brain Trust
http://www.nh.ultranet.com/~lmccann/the_brain_trust.html
Free papers.

Bulk Papers Network
http://www.bulkpapers.com
10,000 free papers, after submission of a paper.

The Cheat Factory
http://cheatfactory.hypermart.com
Free papers.

Cheater.com
http://www.cheater.com
12,000 free papers.

ChuckIII's College Resources
http://www.chuckiii.com
18,000 free papers.

CollegeTermPapers.com
http://www.collegetermpapers.com
Free papers. Submission requested.

Coshe's Reports
http://www.coshe.com
5,000 free papers.

Cow Dung
http://www.cowdung.com
2,000 free papers.

Cyber Essays
http://www.cyberessays.com
Free papers.

Dorian's Paper Archive
http://www.fas.harvard.edu/~dberger/papers/
About 100 free papers.

Downcrap.com
http://members.nbci.com/downcrap
1,000 free papers.

Essay Depot
http://www.essaydepot.com
Free papers.

Essay Edge
http://www.essayedge.com
About 100 free papers.

Essay Organization
http://www.essay.org
1,000 free papers.

Essay Trader
http://essaytrader.totally.net

Essayland.com
http://www.essayland.com
5,000 free papers.

EssayMan
http://come.to/essayman
700 free papers.

EssayWorld.com
http://www.essayworld.com
9,000 free papers.

Free Reports and Essays
http://freeessays.cjb.net
http://www.stormloader.com/freereports/main.htm
About 100 free papers.

Global Essays
http://www.geocities.com/CollegePark/Square/9223
Free papers.

Homework Help
http://www.angelfire.com/ca3/homeworkhelp/papers.html
A handful of free papers.

Homework's Done
http://www.members.aol.com/oohalooo/index2.html
http://www.hometown.aol.com/oohalooo/splash.html
Free papers.

Link Nation
http://www.linknation.com
Free papers.

Net Essays
http://www.netessays.net
16,500 free papers.

Other People's Papers
http://www.oppapers.com
6,000 free papers.

Paper Exchange
http://www.phpcore.com/phpcore/papers/
6,000 free papers.

Planet Papers
http://www.planetpapers.com
2,500 free papers.

School Bytes
http://www.schoolbytes.com
Free papers.

School Sucks
http://www.schoolsucks.com/search
4,600 free papers.

Screw Essays
http://www.screw-essays.com
Free papers.

Screw School
http://www.screwschool.com
Free papers.

Studyworld
http://www.studyworld.com
Free papers.

Term Papers Etc.
http://www.promote.net/papers
Free papers.

Totally Free Papers
http://totally.net
http://www.totallyfreepapers.com

Zakath and Adamooos House of Reports
http://www.geocities.com/Athens/Parthenon/6556/main.html
Free papers.

✓ E.4 SITES OPERATED BY THE PAPER STORE.

The Paper Store has an extensive presence in the papers-for-sale business on the Web, operating several sites, most of which charge $9.85 per page for prewritten papers. The sites may be linked to a common database, though each site advertises a somewhat different total number of papers available.

If you believe a paper may have been purchased from one of The Paper Store sites, visit one or two of the following sites and search by topic. Then compare the several-line summary, the length of the paper, and the number of references with the suspect paper. You may be able to make a probable match on this basis. (Since the text of the papers is unavailable to search engines, you cannot compare the actual texts of the papers unless you purchase a copy of the one you believe matches your suspect paper.)

12000Papers.com
http://www.12000papers.com

15000Papers.com
http://www.15000papers.com

BestPapers.com
http://www.bestpapers.com

Buy Papers.com
http://www.buypapers.com

Essay Finder
http://www.essayfinder.com

Essay Page
http://www.essaypage.com

Essay Site
http://www.essaysite.com

FastPapers.com
http://www.fastpapers.com

Paper Store
http://www.paperstore.net

The Paper Store
http://www.allpapers.com

Papers123.com
http://www.papers123.com

Papers 24-7
http://www.papers24-7.com

Phuck School
http://www.phuckschool.com

Term Papers on File
http://www.termpapers-on-file.com

Thousands of Papers (by The Paper Store)
http://www.termpapers-on-file.com
http://www.introvision.com/top
http://www.paperwriters.com/top

"I can't believe what a huge amount of time this research paper is taking!"

✓ E.5 SITES OPERATED BY THE PAPER EXPERTS.

The company known as The Paper Experts operates several sites, linked to each other, with prewritten papers available for $8.95 per page and custom papers for $18.95 per page.

ABCPapers.com
http://www.abcpapers.com

Apex-Termpapers.com
http://www.apex-termpapers.com

SpeedyPapers.com
http://www.speedypapers.com

Superior Term Papers
http://www.superior-termpapers.com

TermPaper-Experts.com
http://www.termpaper-experts.com

✓ E.6 OTHER SITES SELLING PAPERS.

Commercial sites occasionally use more than one URL (possibly to maximize traffic or determine advertising effectiveness).

A1 Termpapers
http://www.a1-termpaper.com
20,000 papers for sale.

Academic Research Group
http://www.web-marketing.org/cgi-bin/nph-tame.cgi/termpapers/index.tam
Papers for $8 per page.

Academic Term Papers
http://www.academictermpapers.com
http://www.researchcentral.com
http://www.termpaperassistance.com
http://www.termpaperresearch.com
http://www4termpaperassistance.com
30,000 papers for sale at $7 per page.

Accepted Papers
http://www.acceptedpapers.com
Papers for $13 per page.

Bulk Papers Network
http://www.bulkpapers.com
10,000 papers for $15 per paper or trade.

BuyEssays.com
http://buyessays.com
20,000 papers for one $40 membership.

Collegiate Care Research Assistance
http://www.papers-online.com
3,000 papers for sale at $6 per page.

The Doctor
http://www.serve.com/doctor/
Papers for sale at $5 per page and up.

DueNow.com
http://www.eduenow.com
20,000 papers for $20 annual membership fee.

Electronic Library
http://termpapersolutions.com
Papers for sale at $7 per page.

EssayBank
http://www.essaybank.com
Papers for sale or trade.

Essays International
http://www.jerryeden.com/esa
7,000 papers at $5 per paper.

Evil House of Cheat
http://www.cheathouse.comuk/index.html
2,000 papers for an annual $10 membership.

Genius Papers
http://www.geniuspapers.com
"Hundreds" of papers for $10 membership.

Jungle Page
http://www.junglepage.com
$20 per paper.

Knowledge Reports
http://www.knowledge-reports.com
$5 per paper.

Lazy Students
http://www.lazystudents.com
$16 membership for access.

Mad Papers
http://www.madpapers.com
8,000 papers for $8 per year membership.

Papers Inn
http://www.papersinn.com
$12 per page.

Poetry Papers
http://www.poetrypapers.com
$9 per page.

Research Assistance
http://www.research-assistance.com
http://www.4termpaperassistance.com
$8 per page.

Research Papers Online
http://www.ezwrite.com
http://atermpaper.com
$5 per page.

School Paper.com
http://www.schoolpaper.com
$20 membership gains access to database.

Terms n Papers
http://www.termsnpapers.com
Papers for $5 per page plus $15 delivery.

World of Essays
http://server19.hypermart.net/t22/index1.htmlvl

Notes:

Appendix F

Useful Web Links and Articles

This appendix lists several sites that provide examples of official statements and policies, articles of interest relating to plagiarism, and Web sites with relevant content.

✓ F.1 EXAMPLE HONOR CODES.

Stanford University Honor Code
http://www.stanford.edu/dept/vpsa/judicialaffairs/honor_code.htm
More information about the code:
http://portfolio.stanford.edu/100848

University of Michigan, College of Engineering Honor Code
http://www.engin.umich.edu/org/ehc/hcode.html

George Mason University Honor Code
http://www.gmu.edu/facstaff/handbook/aD.html

Presbyterian College Honor Code
http://www.presby.edu/academics/honor_code.htm

Georgia Institute of Technology Honor Code
http://www.honor.gatech.edu/honorcode.html

Duke University Undergraduate Honor Code
http://registrar.duke.edu/ACES/ACES-infobook/honor-code.html

Western Maryland College Honor Code
http://www.wmdc.edu/students/honorcode.html

Tulane University Honor Code
http://www.tulane.edu/~jruscher/dept/Honor.Code.html

"I'm so bummed! Krensky lost my research paper, and I lost the Web address where I got it."

✓ F.2   EXAMPLE STATEMENTS RELATING TO PLAGIARISM AND ACADEMIC INTEGRITY.

UC Davis on Avoiding Plagiarism
http://sja.ucdavis.edu/sja/plagiarism.html
Defines plagiarism, sets down rules, and clarifies usage of sources.

New York University Statement on Plagiarism
http://www.nye.edu/education/studentpolicies/v.html
Outlines principles, student and faculty roles, and sanctions.

Harvard University on Academic Performance
http://www.registrar.fas.harvard.edu/handbooks/student/chapter4/academic_perf
ormance.html
Regulations related to academic behavior (part of the student handbook).

University of Texas on Academic Integrity
http://www.utexas.edu/depts/dos/sjs/academicintegrity.html
Good example of an extensive Web site discussing many areas of student conduct and the importance of honesty.

Rutgers University Policy on Academic Integrity
http://teachx.rutgers.edu/integrity/policy.html
Another very good example of well-developed and extensive policy.

University of Pittsburgh on Academic Integrity
http://www.pitt.edu/~graduate/ai1.html
Another example.

Wichita State University Policy on Academic Integrity
http://www.twsu.edu/~senate/a29.html
Set of definitions, policies, and procedures that may provide useful ideas for other institutions. (Appended to a faculty senate agenda.)

✔ F.3 EXAMPLES SHOWING HOW TO AVOID PLAGIARISM.

Avoiding Plagiarism
http://www.lscc.cc.fl.us/library/guides/plagiarism.htm
Links to several sites with examples and instruction.

Avoiding Plagiarism
http://www.hamilton.edu/academics/resource/wc/avoidingplagiarism.html
General advice with several examples of acceptable and unacceptable use.

Plagiarism: What it is and How to Recognize and Avoid It
http://www.indiana.edu/~wts/wts/plagiarism.html
Examples with analysis of why the acceptable use is acceptable and the plagiarized version is not.

Plagiarism and How to Avoid It
http://users.drew.edu/~sjamieso/plagiarism_examples.html
Informative page with good examples.

The Correct Use of Borrowed Information
http://www.winthrop.edu/english/writingprogram/plagiar.htm
Examples of paraphrasing and incorporating sources.

✔ F.4 OTHER ARTICLES AND SITES OF INTEREST.

Plagiarism in Colleges in USA
http://www.rbs2.com/plag.htm
Lengthy article written by an attorney, covering legal and other aspects of plagiarism.

Cheating 101: Paper Mills and You
http://www.coastal.edu/library/papermil.htm
Informative site relating to cheating and plagiarism.

Center for Academic Integrity
http://www.academicintegrity.org
Resources for academic institutions. Includes ability to search on more than 7,000 Web pages covering academic integrity.

Josephson Institute of Ethics
http://www.josephsoninstitute.org
Materials on ethics, including useful booklet titled *Making Ethical Decisions*.

10 Big Myths about Copyright Explained
http://www.templetons.com/brad/copymyths.html
Clarifies issues relating to the Web and copyright, together with some general information on copyright.

Appendix G

Teaching Ideas for the Cartoons

This appendix includes a description of the cartoons in the book, together with some comments about how each cartoon might be used for stimulating class discussion about plagiarism or one of its aspects. These cartoons may be reproduced for classroom use, subject to the limitations and terms of duplication described in the copyright notice on page *ii*.

✓ G.1 USING THE CARTOONS TO BEGIN A DISCUSSION ABOUT PLAGIARISM.

Plagiarism is a serious issue, with serious consequences. The subject can be upsetting to professors and students alike, and beginning (and sustaining) a discussion about it can be awkward and difficult. The cartoons in this book have been designed to make teaching about and discussing the various aspects of plagiarism much easier for both professor and students. These cartoons offer the following benefits.

➢ They can serve as icebreakers to reduce the tension surrounding the subject. Hostility and resistance will be reduced by an introductory laugh at the situation.

➢ They immediately focus the subject on plagiarism by providing a clear example. In many cases, the cartoons involve specific aspects of plagiarism or areas of student confusion, and they help clear up that confusion.

➤ They can help prevent the discussion from becoming too heavy. Honest students will be able to learn about unintentional plagiarism or about what dishonest students are doing, without feeling like criminals themselves.

➤ They help to create awareness among students that plagiarism is a public issue, that faculty are aware of what is going on (having experience in the area), and are on the alert. Posting a cartoon or two around the classroom will remind students that they are not working in an information vacuum where no one is thinking about the possibility of cheating.

✓ G.2 DISCUSSING THE CARTOONS.

Discussing the cartoons helps the lessons on plagiarism become interactive sessions rather than dry (or browbeating) lectures about cheating. The cartoons are therefore useful as talking stimuli. Discussing them with the class can help clarify various issues, bring up stories from students, even allow some imaginative role-playing. In addition to the ideas specific to each cartoon that follows, here are a few hints that can apply to almost every cartoon:

➤ Many of the cartoons have "audience" characters who are standing or sitting around listening to the plagiarizer say something. In these cases, you might ask your students to put themselves in the position of one of these characters. For example, "If you were the person on the couch, what would you say to this student?"

➤ In cases where the cartoon shows a one-on-one with a professor, you might ask, "How do you think the professor feels here?" Students may be surprised to discover that very few professors enjoy such meetings.

➢ For most of the cartoons, you can remind students that the plagiarizers will eventually have careers. You might ask the students how they would like to have the plagiarizer in the cartoon
as someone in whom they must trust. For example, "How would
you like this person as your lawyer?" (Other professions to substitute include mechanic, supervisor, heart surgeon, dentist, vet-
erinarian, tax preparer, stockbroker, real estate broker.) The
point is that we expect others who serve us to have earned the
credentials they display. Someone who has cheated through
school will not have the same competence as someone who actually did the work, but may still have the same credentials.
Thus, anyone may potentially be a victim of a plagiarizer.

✓ G.3 INDIVIDUAL CARTOON DISCUSSION IDEAS.

If you are planning to use some of these cartoons for classroom illustrations, you might want to read through the comments
on each one here as a means of helping you choose which ones are
most suitable for your topics. While the cartoons have been placed
in the book according to a general connection with the topic under
discussion, you may find a different order preferable.

Cartoon 1. (Page 3)

Two students are looking in the door of a dorm room, where a student inside is working at a computer on her desk. One of the two outside is saying to the other: Must be working on her research
paper. I keep hearing her mumbling, "Edit, copy, edit, paste."

Comments: This cartoon should help students distinguish between the act of
constructing any old product to fulfill a requirement and the act of actually writing a paper, and in the process of researching, thinking, drafting, and so forth,
advancing their education. Discussion might include the purpose of assigning
papers (not merely to give the professor more reading to do!) and how the skills
developed by working through the assignment are the real value of it.

Cartoon 2. (Page 10)

A professor sits at his desk, with stacks of papers on either side and a letter scale in the middle. One
paper is on the scale. Professor: Oh, bad luck! Missed an "A" by a quarter of an ounce! Cutline:
How some students think professors grade papers.

Comments: During classroom testing, many students laughed at this cartoon—
but it was a nervous laughter. In each class, several half-jokingly opined that the

cartoon was rather realistic. These results demonstrate that there is concern among students about the degree of care given to their papers. (A student who has spent fifteen hours writing a four- or five-page paper does not want the effort glanced over in five minutes.) This cartoon, therefore, can provide a good takeoff point for discussing their fears and for explaining how carefully you will be reading their papers. The careful reading promise has another side: the expectation of careful writing. You might ask two questions in order: (1) Do you believe that professors have an obligation to read your papers carefully? (2) Do you believe that students have a corresponding obligation to write papers carefully?

Cartoon 3. (Page 19)

A student is walking across the campus with a university building in the background. The student is holding a cell phone, listening. Voice on the phone: All right, sir. With your coupon for buy two, get one free, that's three causes of the Russian Revolution for $54.95. If you need a somewhat longer paper, you might be interested in our special promotional offer of two additional causes for only $19.95 more!

Comments: This cartoon reveals that the student who purchases a paper neither discovers knowledge nor creates meaning from knowledge. This student does not know whether there were three, five, or sixteen causes of the Russian Revolution, which of the causes were more important than the others, or whether even knowing about those causes has any current significance. Discussion might address the meanings of the word "smart." Is the student a "smart" dresser? Is he getting a "smart" deal with the coupon? Is he being "smart" to buy a paper, especially at a good price? And finally, is this student "smart" (wise or intelligent), or is he going to get any "smarter"? The fact is, this student is cheating himself and limiting his future, and that is hardly a smart thing to do.

Cartoon 4. (Page 27)

A student and a professor are standing together after class. They are holding on to the edges of the same paper. Student: *Plagiarism?* But my roommate gave me permission to use his paper and said I didn't have to cite him. Cutline: Help students distinguish between copyright issues and plagiarism.

Comments: This cartoon is useful for forewarning students that they cannot copy a text simply because they have permission to do so or because the text is in the public domain and is therefore not copyrighted. Students should be told clearly that plagiarism is not the same as copyright infringement. Any collection of words—written, spoken, copyrighted, not copyrighted, sold, or free—can be plagiarized. This cartoon also provides a good visual to inform students that no one else can excuse them from their obligation to cite: Citation is a matter of principle, not of permission. As an aside, you might also mention that virtually the entire Web is copyrighted. Many students mistakenly believe that everything on the Web is in the public domain, hence not copyrighted, and hence copyable without attribution.

Cartoon 5. (Page 33)

Two students at the beach. One student has a notebook computer. Student with computer: Here's one: "My Apology for Cheating on the Ethics Test." Only $19.95. That should get me off the hook. Cutline: If what you do shapes who you are, what kind of person is this?

Comments: This cartoon might be used for a discussion of character, as the cutline suggests. College is a process of becoming someone, and our actions in college influence the kind of person we become. Some questions you might ask related to this cartoon include these: When this student gets married and has a family, what will he answer when his child asks, "Daddy, what did you do in college?" What exactly is this student learning? Would you want to be this student's friend? Why or why not?

Cartoon 6. (Page 39)

Two students are in their dorm room. One is sitting at a computer. Student at the computer: Here's one that's been bought so many times it's *fifty percent off now*. It's called, "Radical Individualism: I Speak for Myself."

Comments: The irony of this cartoon is rich for raising a discussion about how the writing process enables students to discover and express their own ideas. It is sometimes said, "You don't know what you really think about something until you write about it." Writing is thinking. In fact, when carefully done, it usually involves more careful thinking than does either speaking or meditating. Undergraduate students especially are engaged in discovering their own expressive voices, their own ideas, their own analyses of issues, and all these things are developed through writing. You might tell students that if they really understood the benefit of writing assignments, they would eagerly ask for more of them rather than react with dread when such assignments are made. Another possible takeoff point connected to this theme is to start by asking how many students keep journals (or diaries) and why. Journaling is now widely viewed as highly therapeutic and a key to self-understanding.

Cartoon 7. (Page 47)

A professor is standing at the lectern in front of a large class of students (lecture hall size). He is holding a paper in his hand. Professor: I have a paper here, "American Wilderness: Challenge or Threat," but I don't know who wrote it. If any of you knows, please inform me. And that includes all four of you who turned it in.

Comments: Just as there are urban legends circulating through society, there are academic legends circulating through the university. One such legend has it that in a large survey class, nine students turned in identical papers. This cartoon should remind students that the same papers are available for download by anyone, and that there is no guarantee that there will be no duplication. (Even in a class of only 32, the author once received two identical papers—each copied unknowingly from the same third source.)

Cartoon 8. (Page 53)

A student is holding a paper in both hands. *This paper is right on!* I sure wish I'd written it. *Hmm.* Maybe I *will!*

Comments: What is the difference between admiring someone else's paper and claiming to have written it? The following anecdote may offer a stimulus for discussion of this cartoon.

Related anecdote:

I think people mostly plagiarize out of fear of failure or out of laziness. I take pride in my work and would be disgusted with myself if I ever tried to pass someone else's work off as my own. There would be no pride of ownership, which is really important to me.

– Julia Johansen, university senior

For discussing this cartoon, you might ask students why they think some students plagiarize. You might also raise the "pride of ownership" question and ask students if they feel proud of their papers once they have completed them.

Cartoon 9. (Page 58)

A professor is sitting at his desk cleaning his glasses, while a student is gesturing wildly. Student: But you can't give me a B-minus on this paper! The girl who actually *wrote* it got an "A" from her professor just last semester!

Comments: A starting point for discussion might be to ask students why they think the same paper would get such different grades. Do they think that one professor is merely an easier grader? Or do they perhaps think that grading is so subjective that such variation is to be expected? Or that the professor might be biased? After they respond to some questions like these, you might then ask if papers are mere interchangeable commodities or whether a paper that fulfills one requirement well might fail to fulfill another requirement quite as well. This line of questioning could then lead the discussion around to the fact that papers are written to fulfill specific requirements and that a borrowed or stolen paper would unlikely match the requirements as well as a paper written expressly for the purpose.

Cartoon 10. (Page 66)

A professor and a student are standing in front of a blackboard. Student: How did you like my research paper? Professor: I like it better every year.

Comments: A student who hands in a paper copied from any source—Web, roommate, fraternity file, paper mill—has no way of knowing whether the professor has seen the paper before and will remember it. Professors who keep copies of student papers will be able to refresh their memories if a familiar phrase or idea rings a faint bell.

Related anecdote:

My sophomore year I had a freshman come up to me and ask, "Did you have Professor Harris's 104 class?" When I said yes, she asked me if I did the research paper. When I said yes to that as well, she asked me if she could have it. She would have paid me, of course, and changed a few sentences. How stupid can you be? Of course you would have known it was my paper—how many other students have written about the Alar-in-apples scare?

– Julia Johansen, university senior

An important point to remind students about is that copied material, and therefore the evidence of plagiarism, may surface at any time: There is no guarantee that it will ever go away. Another reminder to students might be that they should give professors some credit for having a memory. The memory may be vague at first, but a little diligence might produce the evidence.

Cartoon 11. (Page 70)

A professor stands in his office, holding his nose with one hand. In the other hand, he holds a paper, dangling it over a wastebasket next to his desk as if about to drop the paper in. Two students are outside the office looking in at this scene. One student: Looks like someone turned in another copy of "Deconstructing Michelangelo." Mayfield has *never* liked that paper.

Comments: This cartoon might serve as a good illustration in connection with a discussion of familiarity as a clue to plagiarism. Students might be interested in learning how many papers faculty members grade. Some writing and literature professors grade about 750 papers a year, which, in 20 years, is 15,000 papers. You might estimate how many papers you have graded over the years and share this with students, together with some stories about catching plagiarism through the clue of familiarity.

Cartoon 12. (Page 80)

Before a classroom of students, a professor stands at the lectern. One student has his hand raised and is speaking. Student: You use a software program to check for plagiarized papers? Oh, man, that is *so* sneaky. Isn't that unethical or something?

Comments: This cartoon is a good consciousness-raising discussion starter. Are students aware that professors know that plagiarism exists? Do students realize that professors have tools and techniques for ferreting out plagiarism? In classroom testing, students proved very interested in discussions about plagiarism countermeasures. As has been mentioned in the main text, honest students take great comfort in knowing that professors are concerned about this issue because such concern validates the hard work the honest students do. You might ask the class, "Does the student in this cartoon think that professors do not care about plagiarism or are unwilling or unable to take appropriate steps to counter it?" Or, "Does this student see cheating as a game, with rules about what is and is not fair in the detection of it?" Ask the class members what they think about using various tools for exposing plagiarism.

Cartoon 13. (Page 89)

A professor is sitting at the desk in his office and holding a paper. A student is sitting across on the other side of the desk. Professor: Well, Merkins, I must admit I'm impressed by this paper. In fact, I wish I'd written it myself. No doubt you wish you had, too. Cutline: How *not* to begin a discussion about suspected plagiarism.

Comments: This cartoon may put some fear into students, who will realize that if they cheat, they may be caught and should expect confrontation with the professor. However, the main point here is a message to the professor. As the cutline implies, a direct accusation like this is not the best way to begin a meeting with a student because of the many variables involved even in seemingly clearcut cases. An innocent student, or one who plagiarized inadvertently, could be devastated by this kind of beginning. (See Chapter 5 for suggested methods of proceeding.) To explore this cartoon in a classroom session more deeply, you might ask students how they think the professor discovered the paper was plagiarized. You might also ask them to describe how they think the student feels (assuming that he is guilty).

Cartoon 14. (Page 96)

A professor seated at the desk in his office. A student is seated across from him. The professor holds a paper in his hand. Professor: Parts of this paper are really very good, but I must say that the final third is rather unclear to me. Student: Yeah, I didn't understand that part either...it, er...heh...I...er... mean...*gulp!*

Comments: Of course, one fact this cartoon points out is the embarrassment of looking and feeling foolish when being caught having plagiarized. But more important, it reminds students that the plagiarizer is not learning anything about the subject—or about researching, thinking, or writing. A strategy that successfully preserves the student's ignorance while he or she passes through college will in the end be counterproductive when that student seeks worthy employment.

Cartoon 15. (Page 102)

A professor is sitting at her desk writing. Papers are all over her desk. "Dear Mr. Trent: Since you only *pretended* to write this paper, I only *pretended* to grade it." Cutline: It is probably best to write only, "See me," on papers you suspect have been plagiarized.

Comments: This cartoon may serve as a good starting point for a discussion about the implications of plagiarizing a paper as they relate to the professor. That is, a student who "pretends" to write a paper is trying to fool the professor, is lying to the professor, and is showing no respect for the professor (not to mention the educational process). The student no doubt still expects the professor to put effort into reading and grading the paper, but the student knows the effort will be wasted: None of the comments will matter because the student did not write the paper. Plagiarism is thus a kind of secret thumbing of the nose at the professor. Can professors be blamed, then, when they react with anger at such papers?

Cartoon 16. (Page 113)

A student is standing in the doorway of her apartment with the door open, as if she has just answered the door. Another student is facing her, on the stoop, and holding out a 3½-inch floppy disk (the cartoon mimics holding a measuring cup when asking for a cup of sugar from a neighbor). Neighbor: Hi, Jane. Sorry to bother you, but I'm just now making a paper and I'm all out of words. Could I borrow about 1200?

Comments: This cartoon suggests two routes to a philosophical discussion about writing and plagiarism. First, you might discuss just what "making a paper" is about. Many students view research papers as assembly-line processes where they connect block quotations with minimal commentary: "Jones claims that . . . while Smith asserts . . . but Doe disagrees. . . ." Is there such a thing as a recipe for a paper, as this cartoon suggests? And does that recipe include mixing in a quantity of borrowed words? The second route for discussion (which is more abstract) would be to ask what about words—borrowed or not—makes them useful or makes them into a paper. The idea is that words do not have value or meaning depending on their quantity, but depending on their organization into meaningful statements. The value of creating a research paper lies in the effort it takes to organize words into meaningful expressions. The effort of organization is even more important than the ultimate product because the learning takes place at that point.

Cartoon 17. (Page 120)

A professor is seated at the desk in her office. A stack of papers on one side is 10 to 12 inches high. One paper sits in front of the professor, open, as if she is grading it. Another professor is standing nearby. Seated professor: Work? Well, I have 114 in the class, so that's maybe 75 or 80 different papers to grade.

Comments: This cartoon might stimulate discussion about whether it represents a cynical form of humor. The point of it, however, is that professors are not stupid—experience teaches them how to recognize, or at least suspect, phony papers. And they are alert to the possibility of cheating. Another tack to take with this cartoon is to ask the students to put themselves in the professor's place.

How would they feel about (a) teaching, (b) grading papers, or (c) students, if they faced the probability of plagiarized work in response to their assignments?

Cartoon 18. (Page 127)

A student is standing in a dorm room, reading a letter. His roommate is lying on the couch nearby. Student (holding a paper in one hand and slapping his forehead with the other): *Oh, no! That paper I just turned in is being recalled by the mill! All of the dates are off by 200 years!*

Comments: This cartoon should put students on notice that they are responsible for every flaw in any paper they hand in, and that if they hand in a paper from a mill or any other source, that paper's errors become their errors. You might mention the paper on *Gulliver's Travels* discussed in Chapter 2, Example 2.5.2.1—filled with errors of grammar, spelling, punctuation, historical fact, and even events of the plot. There is no guarantee of quality in an essay simply because it was sold rather than given away; any essay not the student's own can be a risky proposition.

Cartoon 19. (Page 134)

A professor sits in her office at the desk, with a student sitting across. On the desk is an open book. The professor is holding the student's paper as if to say, "Look at the evidence." Student: I meant to put all those paragraphs in quotation marks, but the quote key on my keyboard is broken.

Comments: This cartoon makes what students might call an obviously "lame" excuse. But the cartoon could be used to start a discussion about students' responsibility for their papers. Well in advance of a final version, students should be told that they are personally responsible for the accuracy of punctuation and citation (as well as grammar and so forth) on their papers. Blaming a tutor, a typewriter or computer, a typist, or anyone else will not be accepted. By putting students on notice, you will be less likely to receive high-tech versions of "the dog ate my homework" (the computer crashed, the floppy was blank after I saved the file, my printer broke or ran out of ink, the lab was closed). Another issue to explore with this cartoon might be to ask students what the student should do: make such a pathetic excuse or confess? Do the students think any professor would "buy" this excuse? Is the student helping his case any by trying to talk his way out of the obvious conclusion?

Cartoon 20. (Page 147)

Two faculty members sitting over coffee. One (arms up, holding up two fingers on each hand and wiggling them): Why does Buskin wiggle his fingers when he hands in a paper? Other: Oh, those are just the quotation marks.

Comments: This cartoon makes the point that faculty members talk to each other about students who cheat in their classes. (Faculty members also talk about students who always go beyond the requirements or excel in their work.) Students might be reminded that a reputation for academic dishonesty is not likely to gain them warm letters of recommendation.

Cartoon 21. (Page 159)

A student sits at a table in a library. Next to him is his girlfriend. In front of them are books, papers, and pencils. Student: I should write my own papers more often. I can't believe all the neat stuff I'm learning!

Comments: This cartoon reminds us that students who get into the habit of plagiarizing do not realize what they are missing. Education is about awakening the mind, stimulating curiosity, and engaging interest in focused ways. Research writing opportunities should be welcomed by students interested in real learning. And there is a good starting place for discussion. Some possible questions might be the following: Do you think students who plagiarize are more or less likely to be bored? What do plagiarizers expect to do after they graduate, still lacking the knowledge they supposedly went to college to gain? If students do not develop the ability to find interest in various subjects now, what will they do in their careers when faced with "boring" tasks?

Cartoon 22. (Page 175)

A professor sits in his office at a desk. A student is sitting across. Student: You found my paper at FreePapers.com?! That's *impossible!* I paid good money for it from EssaySales, Inc.!

Comments: One point this cartoon makes is that if you buy a paper, you really do not know what you are getting. To start a discussion on this topic, you might ask students just where they think on-line papers come from. Another starter might be to ask students how the scenario in this cartoon could be accurate? Could a purchased paper also be available free? If a student bought a paper from one site, what would keep him or her from trading it at a site that requires a paper in trade for downloading another paper? Honesty? Integrity? Such questions may lead into a discussion of the character of persons who buy papers. In what way is their character being formed?

Cartoon 23. (Page 186)

A student is sitting at his desk with a stack of books on the side. He has a pen in hand, and a look of stress. Titles include: Downloads R Us, Genuine Fake Papers, Copy Our Stuff, Cheat Inc., A-1 Download. Caption: I can't believe what a huge amount of time this research paper is taking!

Comments: The student in this cartoon displays the irony of working hard at being dishonest in order to save himself from having to work hard at being honest. What exactly will this student learn, and what will he become by this process? Dishonesty may be somewhat less work than honesty, but is it less stressful? This cartoon might once again be an opportunity to mention that the plagiarist is constructing possibly permanent evidence of cheating that might be discovered at any time.

Cartoon 24. (Page 192)

Three students are sitting in a lounge. One: I'm so bummed! Krensky lost my research paper, and I lost the Web address where I got it.

Comments: This cartoon reminds students (in a roundabout way) to save a final copy of every paper, together with their drafts, notes, and research materials at least until they get their papers back. When a paper occasionally disappears somewhere between the student's hand and the professor's, the professor will expect another copy, or at the very least, a draft and evidence of the writing process. If a student says that not a shred of evidence remains ("I threw it all away"), the professor might be suspicious.

References

Arnett, J. (2000). Emerging adulthood: A theory of development from the late teens through the twenties. *American Psychologist, 55,* 469-480.

Bergman, M. (2000). The deep web: surfacing hidden value. [on-line white paper]. Bright Planet. Retrieved August 15, 2000 from the World Wide Web: http://www.completeplanet.com/Tutorials/DeepWeb/contents04.asp

Bjaaland, P., & Lederman, A. (1973). The detection of plagiarism. *The Educational Forum, 37,* 201-206.

Burrell, B. (1997). *The words we live by.* New York: Free Press. pp. 235-40.

Bushweller, K. (1999, March). Digital deception: the Internet makes cheating easier than ever. *Electronic School,* pp. A18+.

Clayton, M. (1997, October 27). Term papers at the click of a mouse. *The Christian Science Monitor.* [online newspaper]. Retrieved August 18, 2000 from the World Wide Web: http://www.csmonitor.com/durable/1997/10/27/feat/learning.1.html

Ekman, P. (1992). *Telling lies: clues to deceit in the marketplace, politics, and marriage.* New York: Norton.

Emery, D. (2000, January 13). The curse of frankenchicken. Urban Legends and Folklore. Retrieved October 15, 2000 from the World Wide Web: http://urbanlegends.about.com/science/urbanlegends/library/weekly/aa010500a.htm

Ferguson, C. (2000). Free will: an automatic response. *American Psychologist, 55,* 762-763.

Ford, C. (1996). *Lies! lies! lies! The psychology of deceit.* Washington, D.C.: American Psychiatric Press.

Foreign students at Southern Cal. found disproportionately among cheaters. (1998, December 11). *Chronicle of Higher Education,* p. A61.

Hausman, C. (1999). *Lies we live by: defeating doubletalk and deception in advertising, politics, and the media.* New York: Routledge.

Howard, R. (1999). The new abolitionism comes to plagiarism. In L. Buranen & A. Roy (Eds.), *Perspectives on plagiarism and intellectual property in a postmodern world* (pp. 87-95). New York: State University of New York Press.

Kelly, R. (2000, January 24). Are you sure those words are your own? Retrieved July 29, 2000 from the World Wide Web: http://www.bufa.org/issues/plagiarism.htm

Lieberman, D. (1998). *Never be lied to again.* New York: St. Martin's.

Maramark, S. & Maline, M. (1993, August). Academic dishonesty among college students. *Issues in Education,* pp. 3-14. Retrieved August 7, 2000, from SIRS Knowledge Source on the World Wide Web: http://www.researcher.sirs.com

Mayfield, K. (1999, December 13). Catching digital cheaters. Reposted in Catching digital cheaters. *Educational Cyber Playground.* [online article] Retrieved July 29, 2000 from the World Wide Web: http://www.edu-cyberpg.com/Teachers/plagiarism.html

References

McCabe, D. & Drinan, P. (1999, October 15). Toward a culture of academic integrity. *Chronicle of Higher Education*. p. B7.

McCabe, D. & Trevino, L. (1993, September/October). Academic dishonesty: honor codes and other contextual influences. *Journal of Higher Education*, 64:5 pp.522-538.

Nickerson, R. (1999). How we know—and sometimes misjudge—what others know: imputing one's own knowledge to others. *Psychological Bulletin, 125*, 737-759.

Porter, S. (2000). Credibility assessment, criminal responsibility, and competency to stand trial. Dalhousie University. [on-line course notes]. Retrieved September 5, 2000 from the World Wide Web: http://www.acsweb.ucis.dal.ca/psych/3224p3

Reed, T. (1999, October 19). Rutgers, Columbia study shows cheating on the rise. Studentadvantage.com [online article] Retrieved August 18, 2000 from the World Wide Web:
http://www.studentadvantage.com/article_story/0,1075,c0-i0-t0-a17135,00.html

Renard, L. (1999). Plagiarism & the net. Retrieved July 31, 2000 from the World Wide Web: http://www.peaklearn.com/article2.html

Roig, M. (1997, Winter). Can undergraduate students determine whether text has been plagiarized? *The Psychological Record, 47*, pp. 113-123. Retrieved August 9, 2000 from Infotrac Expanded Academic ASAP database.

Ryan, J. (1998, December). Student plagiarism in an online world. *ASEE Prism Online*. [online journal]. Retrieved August 21, 2000 from the World Wide Web: www.asee.org/prism/december/html/student_plagiarism_in_an_onlin.htm

Schneider, A. (1999, January 22). Why professors don't do more to stop students who cheat. *Chronicle of Higher Education*, 45, A8.

Shoemaker, T. (1997, May 28). Investigation deception cues: a rubric for detecting lies. Retrieved September 5, 2000 from the World Wide Web:
http://www.multipull.com/twacasefile/cue.html

Standler, R. (2000, October 28). Plagiarism in colleges in USA. Retrieved November 3, 2000 from the World Wide Web: http://www.rbs2.com/plag.htm

Stebelman, S. (1998, September). Cybercheating: dishonesty goes digital. *American Libraries*, 29:8, pp.48-50.

Stroffolino, M. (1997). How to plagiarize papers off the Internet. Retrieved August 12, 2000 from the World Wide Web:
http://www.orbits.com/~maria/plagarize.html

Vrij, A. (2000). *Detecting lies and deceit: the psychology of lying and implications for professional practice*. New York: John Wiley.

Western Maryland College. (2000, July 7). Questions about the WMC honor code. Retrieved September 12, 2000 from the World Wide Web:
http://www.wmdc.edu/students/honorcode.shtml

White, E. (1999). Student plagiarism as an institutional and social issue. In L. Buranen & A. Roy (Eds.), *Perspectives on plagiarism and intellectual property in a postmodern world* (pp. 205-210). New York: State University of New York Press.

Wiggins, G. (1993). *Assessing student performance*. San Francisco: Jossey-Bass.

Wurman, R. (1989). *Information anxiety*. New York: Doubleday.

Index

Index